"*Motioning the Way* is a compelling antidote to the rush and superficiality of preparing for Christmas. It has great depth in challenging us to encounter fully the One born in a stable. Andrew Krauss combines his theological expertise with experience of working with this material in a local church, asking us to consider time and give time in our Advent journey."

—DAVID WILKINSON,

Professor, Durham University

"A scientist-priest reflects on the Advent season. In *Motioning the Way*, the author, with his unique background as an English scientist-priest married to a German Lutheran theologian, delivers a deeply insightful examination of the Advent season, so beloved in both English and German culture. Refreshingly distinct from a mere devotional text, this volume delves into profound theological issues bridging themes of creation, redemption, hope and eschatology, understood through the liturgical season of Advent. Here the reader will find an in-depth treatment of key Advent figures such as St. John the Baptist and the Blessed Virgin Mary, and the traditional O Antiphons. In this short volume, the author brings together insights from the scriptures, the Church Fathers, contemporary theologians and writers as well as his own scientific background, making it a rich, multifaceted study. Overall, *Motioning the Way* is a remarkable resource that offers fresh theological insights into this liturgical season."

—DAVID HAMID,

Retired Bishop, Church of England

"Andrew Krauss obviously has a gift for setting our minds in motion when it comes to theological reflections, as he has done in this book. These texts are an important and inspiring correction to the more and more superficial, extravagant, and commercialized versions of the Advent Journey. His twenty-four Advent reflections resonate the biblical 'breadth and length and height and depth' to which the letter to the Ephesians refers (Eph 3:18). His texts are filled with many historical, etymological, and theological references, opening up new doors and new windows and still keeping the journey in motion. Another of his concerns is that the Advent journey is not an individual journey, but a communal one. It is a journey together 'with all the saints.' For me personally, reading the last seven reflections was particularly inspiring. In my Norwegian, Lutheran liturgical tradition (The Church of Norway) the 'O Antiphons' are not often invoked in the Advent season. The introduction to these texts were a special Advent gift to me, and I strongly recommend this book."

—TOR BERGER JØRGENSEN,

Former Bishop, Church of Norway

"From experiences as a pastor, church executive, posts at university, from working for the United Evangelical Lutheran Church of Germany, and now for GNC/LWF I personally would see this book as theologically well-reflected *Erbauungsliteratur* in the best sense of the word—that accepts God and religion as a reality, that supports one's own thinking about aspects of traditional, still valid terms like Advent, that starts from serious exegetical and biblical insight, that offers personal Christian insight of a learned man to be thought about, and that points at basic kinds of patterns of human and Christian life and thinking."

—ANDREAS OHLEMACHER,

German National Council, Lutheran World Federation

"This is an excellent resource for encouraging discipleship in Advent. Here is an invitation to think deeply and consider carefully the gracious gift of God coming among us. I found it stimulating, spiritually profound, and a real challenge—exactly what Advent should offer."

—HELEN CAMERON,

Former President, Methodist Conference

"With the Christmas Festival largely lost to commercialism, it is more important than ever that we guard and treasure the preceding Advent season. This book provides informative and stimulating material for daily reading as a way into understanding the liturgy, the doctrine, and the message of one of the richest times in the Christian year."

—BARRY ORFORD,

Former Member, Community of the Resurrection, Mirfield

Motioning the Way

Motioning the Way

A Journey Through the Breadth and Depth of Advent

ANDREW KRAUSS

RESOURCE *Publications* • Eugene, Oregon

MOTIONING THE WAY
A Journey Through the Breadth and Depth of Advent

Resource Publications
An Imprint of Wipf and Stock Publishers
199 W. 8th Ave., Suite 3
Eugene, OR 97401

www.wipfandstock.com

PAPERBACK ISBN: 979-8-3852-7742-1
HARDCOVER ISBN: 979-8-3852-7743-8
EBOOK ISBN: 979-8-3852-7744-5

VERSION NUMBER 04/01/26

With deep gratitude to all those who encouraged me
to commit this to writing.

Contents

Acknowledgements

I would like to express my gratitude to all those who first encouraged me to commit this to writing, and to Helen Cameron, David Hamid, Tor Berger Jørgensen, Andreas Ohlemacher, Barry Orford, and David Wilkinson for reading and endorsing the final draft of the text itself.

Preface

Why have I written this book? Indeed, why did I consider writing it in the first place?

Advent is a far broader and deeper season than it is often given credit for, and has certainly always been a season that has had a very deep impact on me, ever since I first became involved in the life of the church. This steadily increased as I went through the process of exploring a call to, and subsequently training for, ordained ministry. Being a parish priest for the majority of my time since ordination opened up yet further possibilities for exploring the season, both through sermons and through Advent study or reflection groups. During these years in particular I started to appreciate more deeply *why* it was that this season seemed, to me at least, to contain such a sense of depth and richness.

I am not the sort of person who has "favorites"—no more a favorite season of the liturgical year than a favorite biblical verse. Even when asked what my favorite film, book or food is, I struggle to decide what would even be in my top ten. Where Advent is concerned, it was simply that there was a degree of fascination involved that I found drew me into the season in a way I couldn't at first have described, an experience I have also, incidentally, found with the Gospel of John (but that, clearly, is a subject for another book).

My enthusiasm for the season seemed to be picked up by various parishioners and, on some occasions, comments were made along the lines of "you really ought to write something down and publish on this, something like an Advent reflection book." Suggestions along these lines persisted over time, so I eventually decided to respond to them, and it is with both joy and much gratitude that I do so.

The first thing that probably springs to most people's minds when they hear the word Advent, apart from it being basically December, is the so-called Advent calendar. I say "so-called" because in reality the images that you find behind the doors of a standard "Advent" calendar are not really Advent images at all, but rather *Christmas-come-early* images. Indeed, it is also the case that many, if not most of these correspond to images associated with a secular celebration of Christmas, with only a few actually corresponding to the biblical narrative.

When I got married, I acquired a German side to my family, and in Germany Advent is a very big season indeed. The calendars can often be far grander and more varied, but still largely, like the markets that will appear in all built-up areas in some cases before Advent has even quite begun, indicative of an early Christmas. Some Advent calendar manufacturers are alert to this issue and you can get calendars that, instead of having pictures or chocolates, actually have daily biblical quotations that are, to an extent, picked to have some specific relevance to Advent rather than Christmas.

This is certainly a step towards treating Advent with the distinctiveness and respect that it deserves, in its own right, as the intensely rich and compact season that it is. In many ways it is lamentable that there are only four Sundays within it, and there was a time in the church's history when Advent was the same length as Lent. It would not be hard to fill extra Sundays with potent Advent themes, simply because there are so many of them, and all of them distinctive from that of Christmas. One notable and important point, however, is that the major themes that are specific to Advent tend to be what many might call "abstract," in the sense that they cannot really be captured by one static picture or image, and hence the difficulty with Advent calendars. Such themes include hope, judgement, the consummation or end of all things, the nature and place of prophecy, patience, alertness . . . among many others.

In what follows it is my aim to present a progressive unfolding of many of these themes in the form of a set of developing reflections. The fact that there are twenty-four reflections in total is purely due to the fact that I originally drafted one per day during the Advent season in 2024, and it should be emphasized at once that this is certainly *not* intended to mean that anyone must read one per day (though some readers may of course choose to do so if time allows). Furthermore, this book is not necessarily intended to be confined to a December reading, since Advent is, very importantly, theologically relevant to the *whole* year, not just to the run-up to Christmas.

I have tried, in as far as it is possible and practical, to make it such that the theme of a given reflection naturally follows on from where that of the previous one left off, but there are inevitably some section breaks at certain points, especially when it comes to incorporating the traditional "O Antiphons" that some readers may already be familiar with. Also, although there will be several references to scriptural texts in the course of these reflections, it is not the case that each one comes with its own particular biblical verse. This is partly because it is the *thematic connections* between various parts of Scripture that is of principal interest here, but also because the emphasis is as much on the overall *texture* of the season as it is on any accompanying or supporting text. Just as a quick note, however, wherever scripture is quoted in what follows the translation is taken from the NRSV Anglicized Edition.

Conveniently enough, it happened to be Advent 2024 when I finally got around actually to committing this to writing, and by an interesting coincidence this was a year in which Advent Sunday fell exactly on 1st December. My original drafting of the reflections was therefore able to stay in step, in one sense, with the Advent calendar, but the goal remains to explore what is particular to the season itself, not only avoiding an early Christmas but also bringing out the enduring relevance of Advent to the *whole* of the liturgical year. Without the theological *foundations* that are to be explored and re-explored each Advent, it is fair to say that Christmas would neither have occurred full stop—certainly not in the manner that we know now—nor could it truly be appreciated for what it really signifies.

Before delving into the reflections themselves, however, I first present a brief but important theological introduction to the nature of the season overall, since this will provide a context for the overall holding together of many of the themes that follow, including the various links and relations between them.

Theological Introduction

The Deep Grounding of Advent

In order to consider the theological underpinning of the season we should of course start with the root of the word "Advent" itself, from the Latin *ad* (to or towards) and *venire* (to come). Advent is therefore a time of reflecting on the nature of God's *coming towards* us, so that we might *also come* to deepen our appreciation of what is involved in God being with us and among us.

This is the most obvious sense in which Advent naturally precedes Christmas, pre-empting God's coming among us in Christ. However, as ought to be equally obvious and will become evident in what follows, Advent also continues its relevance post-Christmas. In certain respects, Advent could be considered the most theologically foundational season, not least because it effectively draws us to consider the dynamic grounding upon which the very *possibility* of our faith and relation with God is based. It is fitting therefore that the season also marks the beginning of a new church year, providing a time for reconsidering our *roots* in a manner that (hopefully) builds on the reflections of previous years as we grow and mature in our journey of faith and discipleship.

As will become apparent in these reflections, Advent touches on a wide variety of themes, and in order for a deeper sense of connection to be made between them it is important to start by expanding the foundational principle highlighted by the root meaning of Ad-vent just mentioned. As a season rooted in the idea of a *divine motioning towards* creation, Advent emphasizes a *dynamic* lying at the core of reality. I choose the word "motioning" deliberately here, since it carries with it a sense of indicating and directing.

In emphasizing such motioning Advent highlights *activity*—the "verb" that carries the action, as it were. It is often said that in order for a sentence to classify as a sentence it must contain a verb, even if the sentence is a one-word imperative such as, to pick an obvious Advent example, "Come!" The verb is, on this viewpoint, necessary in order for the sentence to make sense *as* a sentence. This emphasis on the underlying dynamic becomes all the more important if, as many theologians have suggested, we view God not as "*a* being" somehow among other beings, but rather as pure and complete Being in and of Itself, and therefore the self-sufficient Source of all creation. The key verb then naturally becomes the verb *to be*, which has some immediate advantages. For instance, God's *Infinite* nature could be paralleled with the *infinitive* form of the verb, or what we normally think of as the *name* of the verb—TO BE. This is the source of the most fundamental activity of all, that of simply being, unconstrained by any specific context or contingency. This infinitive quality reflects the *infinite self-sufficiency* of divinity.

From and through this Infinite Being a finite creation is *motioned* into being. Not only that, but this same creation is given a certain orientation and sense of meaning in conscious life, bringing to mind a sense of *relation* between Infinite Being and finite beings—between the infinite and infinitive quality of the divine "TO BE" and the finitude of creaturely existence. The word "existence" is especially appropriate here, as applied to finite creatures. We can write this word more helpfully as ex-sistence, which shows the Latin origin of the word. It means something coming *out of* or *from* (*ex-*) that which in some respect allows it to take a "stand" (*sistere*), in the sense of affording it a certain stability. So it is, theologically speaking, both *out of* and *upon* the foundational and inherently self-sufficient stability of God (as Infinite Being) that our *contingent* stability, our ex-sistence, is ultimately derived and grounded. That sentence may merit re-reading briefly, as it is a key theological starting point.

It is here that we come closer to the root of what it is to be an Advent people. God, as Infinite Being, motions finite creation *into* existence and further motions *towards* that existence in self-revealing to it in some respect. A key aspect of this self-revealing occurs in the creation of a *context* for the reception and appreciation of such revealing among us, which further *enables us* in some respect to motion back towards God in response. Ultimately this is something that can only be done *fully* by Christ, as both divine and human, and hence the profound meaning and importance of the Christian story and message concerning the Incarnation, God's coming among us in human nature, taking human flesh and form.

Considering our finite, creaturely context, *our* "motioning," physically and mentally, is obviously and inevitably constrained by the spatial, temporal, and material nature of our existence. Nevertheless, that finite creation, that particular context according to which our creaturely reception occurs, *by* and *in* which our capacity for response to God is both formed and informed, sets the stage for the outworking of God's self-revealing. This "stage" may at times seem tense, but it *qualifies*, in certain key respects, the outward, creative expression of the Infinite TO BE upon which its very existence depends. In its entirety it effectively acts as a complex *lens*, to pick perhaps the most accessible metaphor, by which some aspect of the divine light can be appreciated in accordance with the finite nature of humanity. In other words, the created context in question gives the *living result* of God's motioning towards creation—and especially towards us—a particular "feel." That feel is, in the most general terms, what Advent draws us towards and encourages us to explore further.

I mentioned that the verb plays a vital part in any meaningful sentence, and it may be helpful here quickly to remind ourselves that the manner in which a verb functions in the context of a particular sentence occurs in two ways. First and foremost, the verb is *conjugated*. In other words, it is made to fit a particular context both in terms of tense—expressing a specific relation to and within *time*—and, where appropriate, in terms of the relation to the subject and the object of the sentence. Additionally, there is the question of the so-called "mood" in which the verb is expressed. Does it indicate what *is* actually happening or *has* actually happened or *will* definitely at some point happen, or does it describe something that *might* be the case? Is it perhaps an imperative, a command like the aforementioned one-word sentence "Come!"? These considerations can clearly have a significant effect, or even affect, with respect to the expression of context. If we use this by way of analogy in considering the outworking of the divine TO BE in bringing about the created context that we feel and experience, then we could well say that the form of the "conjugation" in question is predominantly established on our behalf, in the sense that we are born into it. It is made manifest through the creating and sustaining of *the particular context* in which we consciously experience what it is to exist—this particular universe, this specific feel, this situation-related tension, this flavor of reality.

But there is still another manner in which the activity of a verb can be qualified in a sentence, namely by the use of *adverbs*, describing something of the *way in which* the activity in question works itself out in practice. For example, does it occur slowly or suddenly, overtly or covertly, straightforwardly or rather more cryptically? These questions in particular will prove significant to the reflections that follow. Furthermore, there are also respects in which *our* active (albeit secondary) response to God's primary motioning and "coming towards" us can make its *own* particular qualification in this adverbial sense. In other words, *we* may somehow influence the manner in which the coming or motioning works itself out and the "feel" of how it does so. We may do so in a sense that is both qualif*ied* by God's *primary*, self-revealing motioning towards us and qualify*ing* through our *secondary*, responsive motioning towards God. In this sense, to be an Ad-vent people is also to be an ad-verbial people, since we are granted a capacity for cooperating in the process of being *oriented towards that Infinite TO BE* in whom "we live and move and have our being" (Acts 17:28).

It is then out of this *dynamic* way of looking at the foundation of our reality as-a-whole that a whole host of truly *Advent* concepts emerge, since they are all involved in the feel or texture of what it is to be an adverbial, Advent people, a people held within a greater narrative than that of our individual lives. The narrative contours in which Advent is especially interested are those incorporating the sense of a *collective history* and a *prospective, shared future*. Immediately we hit here on the fact that *time* is in itself a key Advent concept. There is the question of how we consider and interpret time more generally, and also the "signs" of the times more specifically. With this comes questions of hope and expectation, but also of memory and repentance, which in turn produces questions relating to judgement and to what theologians call eschatology, a term pointing to the idea of the final consummation of creation in the Life of the Trinity and according to the purpose of God. This relates to what Ephesians 1:10 refers to as "a plan for the fullness of time," and, once again, time is a key concept here.

These major themes can, in turn, act as points of departure for a longer list of more particular and detailed Advent considerations that the commercially produced Advent calendar won't come anywhere near. It is only out of a more theologically foundational consideration of the *contours of the reality* we experience that the breadth and the depth of interconnection that we find in this rich season can more appreciably be explored. So, with that in mind, it is time to begin with the reflections themselves.

Reflection 1

Motioning and Coming

The Greek philosopher Aristotle, who was deeply interested in the subject of causation, put forward the idea of a primary cause that was itself uncaused, and to which everything that was caused is ultimately to be drawn. This was known as the Prime Mover or the Unmoved Mover. This Prime Mover related entirely to itself—in other words it was self-sufficient—and could be thought of, if you like, in terms of an entirely independent mind, not contingent upon anything outside of itself.

No prizes for guessing that this concept would later be picked up by philosophers and theologians, and especially so by the famous medieval theologian, Thomas Aquinas. Without going into too much detail, the concept is on principle a rich and potentially useful one, as long as we avoid one particular danger. Specifically, we need to avoid thinking of a primary cause simply as a first event that sets the universe in motion, via the isolated decision or conviction of some divine rationality, but which otherwise has no enduringly meaningful or developing relation with its creation, and no active involvement within it. That would be a form of Deism, a belief in a deity who is not considered actively involved with creation other than in the act of bringing it about, which is certainly not in keeping with Christian doctrine. It is far removed from the God of self-revelation through the scriptures and in the Person of Jesus Christ, not least because a deistic viewpoint does not generally accept the idea of specific revelation.

If, however, we consider God as the One who always takes the *primary initiative*, as the One whose "moving" or "motioning" not only brings creation into existence but also sustains it, reveals something of the divine Selfhood to it, and ultimately redeems it and renews it in Christ, then we have very much the God of Christianity. Creaturely response to God is then a *secondary initiative*, but one which is allowed a distinctive form of freedom by the love and grace of God, and not least because a key aspect of the aforementioned "plan for the fullness of time" was the taking up of human nature in union with that of divinity in the Incarnation. The final resting place, as it were, is then a participation in the Life of God or, in Christian terminology, the Life of the Trinity. This is made quite clear in the development of John's Gospel in particular, and by the well-known phrase from the Second Letter of Peter that we are to "become participants in the divine nature" (2 Pet 1:4). Further pointers towards this idea can be found in 1 Corinthians 15:20–28 and throughout Ephesians 1, and also in the great declaration of Colossians 1:15–20, for those who may wish to look them up at this point.

Clearly the previous paragraph has greatly compacted a huge amount of Christian teaching into a very short space, which can be developed in a great number of ways, as we can also see happening in the biblical witness. It does, however, hold open the broadest possible viewpoint regarding God's motioning *of* creation into existence, and of God's coming and motioning *towards* creation, and towards *us* more specifically as bearers in some key respect of divine "image" (Gen 1:26). This includes giving us the *freedom* and the *capacity*—indeed, our freedom in this case is specifically *in* our capacity—to make a response back to God, whether by prayer, by obedience to commandments, by a discernment of vocation, or by a will to seek the signs of a new creation in Christ. God's primary initiative in motioning towards us enables and evokes our creaturely response, which in turn can be drawn back to God and into the Life of the Trinity.

This flow from God, back to God, is also something echoed at various points in the biblical witness, such as Isaiah 55:10–11 . . .

> For as the rain and the snow come down from heaven, and do not return there until they have watered the earth, making it bring forth and sprout, giving seed to the sower and bread to the eater, so shall my word be that goes out from my mouth; it shall not return to me empty, but it shall accomplish that which I purpose, and succeed in the thing for which I sent it.

A relation in this case to the Word in Christ is likely to be fairly clear here to Christian readers, and the final words may also remind us of a famous Advent text, specifically Isaiah 43:19, "I am about to do a new thing; now it springs forth, do you not perceive it? I will make a way in the wilderness and rivers in the desert."

This is the great, broad-brushstroke vision that is set before us to contemplate afresh at the start of each liturgical year, reminding us both of the roots and of the bigger picture. Here it is certainly something of a springboard for reflection on the "days to come," which is itself a fitting phrase for Advent. Advent Sunday texts are often chosen specifically on the basis that they contain the word "come." To give some examples from the principal service readings for Advent Sunday in the Church of England's *Common Worship Lectionary*, consider the following (my italics highlighting the word *come*) . . .

Isaiah 2:1–5 contains phrases and sentences such as, "In days to *come* the mountain of the Lord's house shall be established as the highest of the mountains, and shall be raised above the hills; all the nations shall stream to it" (verse 2). It continues with, "Many peoples shall *come* and say, '*Come*, let us go up to the mountain of the Lord, to the house of the God of Jacob'" (verse 3), and then a little later, "O house of Jacob, *come*, let us walk in the light of the Lord!" (verse 5).

In Isaiah 64:1–9 we hear the words, "O that you would tear open the heavens and *come* down, so that the mountains would quake at your presence" (verse 1), and later on a petition to God to "consider, we are all your people" (verse 9). The sense of being *together* in this arena of God's motioning towards us is another important dimension to Advent.

In Jeremiah 33:14–16 we hear that, "The days are surely *coming*, says the LORD, when I will fulfil the promise I made to the house of Israel and the house of Judah" (verse 14), and with some potent words to finish the reading in question, namely, "The LORD is our righteousness" (verse 16).

From Psalm 80 we hear, "Give ear, O Shepherd of Israel, you who lead Joseph like a flock! . . . Stir up your might, and *come* to save us!" (verses 1–2).

In Psalm 122:1 there is the famous declaration, "I was glad when they said to me, 'Let us go to the house of the LORD!'" (which is basically a case of "*Come*, let us go").

In Romans 13:11–14 we hear how the coming of the LORD, specifically now in Christ, means that "salvation is nearer to us now than when we became believers" (verse 11), which is a great reminder of the *journey* believers take in the faith and that Advent too is a season of journeying, and doing so together.

In 1 Thessalonians 3:9–13 we are reminded of "the *coming* of our Lord Jesus with all his saints" (verse 13). This again emphasizes the communal aspect involved.

In Matthew 24:36–44 we hear that "as the days of Noah were, so will be the *coming* of the Son of Man. For as in those days . . . they knew nothing until the flood *came* and swept them all away, so too will be the *coming* of the Son of Man" (verses 37–39). We also hear the exhortation, "Keep awake therefore, for you do not know on what day your Lord is *coming* . . . if the owner of the house had known in what part of the night the thief was *coming*, he would have stayed awake . . . Therefore you also must be ready, for the Son of Man is *coming* at an unexpected hour" (verses 42–44). This passage extends to other Advent themes, such as alertness, expectation, and suddenness, which will be developed in subsequent reflections.

In Mark 13:24–37 we hear this echoed afresh in the words "they will see "the Son of Man *coming* in clouds" with great power and glory" (verse 26), and then in a repeat of the fact that "you do not know when the time will *come*" (verse 33), and again, "you do not know when the master of the house will *come* . . . he may find you asleep when he *comes* suddenly" (verses 35–36).

Luke 21:25–36 makes an even sharper point in mentioning the "fear and foreboding of what is *coming* upon the world, for the powers of the heavens will be shaken. Then they will see "the Son of Man *coming* in a cloud" with power and great glory" (verses 26–27). This is followed by another reference to "redemption is drawing near" (verse 28) and the collective nature of the concern is further emphasized in the words "it will *come* upon all who live on the face of the whole earth" (verse 35). This further brings in the theme of shaking up, which will also be the subject of a subsequent reflection.

These officially suggested readings for use on Advent Sunday, over a three-year cycle, set the scene and the tone for a fresh contemplation at the start of a new church year. They highlight many distinctive dimensions to the concept of God's "coming," and in so doing prepare us to encounter afresh the breadth, the depth, and the challenge of the Advent season as a collective people. We will see many of the other concepts noted among these readings developed in the reflections that follow, but just to finish for this opening reflection, what about *our* response and *our* coming, of which we hear some explicit exhortations in the Old Testament readings just cited from Isaiah 2 and Psalm 122? If we were asked to pick just one biblical exhortation for us to "come" as a scene-setter for our Advent journey together, then I for one would choose those famous words from John 1:39, when Jesus says to the first disciples to follow him, "*Come* and see."

Reflection 2

Opening and Revelation

When we hear words such as moving, motioning, or coming, we are likely to imagine some kind of *way* or *path* according to which this happens, which already brings to mind the famous Advent phrase about the way being prepared in the wilderness by John the Baptist—a subject for a later reflection. Even when the motioning in question is being understood in the more metaphorical sense of *bringing into existence*, and of *relating* in some way to and with the creation that results, there must still be some "way" according to which this happens.

Christian teaching and biblical witness expand on this with the idea that such motioning is *from* the Father, *through* the Son *in the power of* the Holy Spirit. With regard to the Son in particular, we hear that "All things came into being through him" (John 1:3) and that "in him all things in heaven and on earth were created . . . all things have been created through him and for him" (Col 1:16). A little later in Colossians we also hear that, "through him God was pleased to reconcile to himself all things" (Col 1:20) and, fittingly, Christ then describes himself as "the way" in John 14:6.

Clearly, the way in question needs to lie *open* in order to afford the lively relation between Creator and creatures that lies at the heart of the Advent journey. We use the word "open" in many different ways. We ask people to open their hearts or minds to something. We may describe someone as an open person or coming from an open tradition. We may point someone towards a job opening, or consider that a possibility more generally has been opened up. We may also talk about opening channels of communication with someone, and this brings us closer to a connection between the idea of opening and that of *revelation*. In order for revelation to be possible even *on principle* two things must be the case. Firstly, we must be created and formed such that we have the *capacity* to receive something of God's self-revealing, which may well play a major role in what it is to bear the "image" of God noted in Genesis 1:26–27. Secondly, despite there being a fundamental distinction between divinity and humanity, there must be a *sufficient relation* to allow some sense of nearness or resonance between the two, such that something *of* God can be revealed in finite and comprehensible terms. This too must surely pertain to that image-bearing quality in which humanity is made.

In biblical literature the concept of revelation is sometimes accompanied by reference to the *opening* of a portal in the heavens, such as in Revelation 4:1, and we might compare this with Jesus describing himself as the "gate" in John 10:7–9. Once again, Jesus is the one *through* whom something is able to occur, by and in whom some opening or unique possibility is *afforded*. The psychologist, J. J. Gibson, is credited with coining the now quite commonly used word "affordance" to describe a resonant relation between a creature and its environment. An affordance is basically a conceptual expression used to describe how creatures perceive openings or possibilities for action in their environment—what that environment will and will not support given the nature of the creature in question's specific embodiment. Moreover, as creatures capable of long-term planning, human beings especially can, and should, use their particular capacity to discern what can and cannot be supported in the longer term, being as careful and responsible as possible, especially in an age of environmental crisis.

The concept of an affordance is useful, I think, in talking about revelation. We are afforded a *specific*—i.e. pertaining to a capacity inherent in our *species*—form of relation with God in accordance with God's self-revealing. There is a *resonance* of relation between divinity and humanity, which Christians believe to be in perfect union in Christ. It is also the basis on which we speak of the Word, the *Logos* in the Greek text,[1] both in terms of scriptural revelation *and* in terms of Christ himself, and should therefore expect the scriptures to point towards the Christ in whom the relation between divinity and humanity is one of full union. We need, however, responsibly to distinguish the *sense* in which, on the one hand, we refer to the Word as working somehow in and among the many *words* of the scriptural texts—including the significant imperfection of human involvement with them—and that, on the other hand, in which we refer to the Word as "in the beginning with God" and also *as* God, and furthermore as becoming flesh in the full perfection of Christ (John 1:1–2, 14).

We also need to remember that, while the common use of the term affordance refers simply to a creature's relation with its environment, to apply the term to the concept of the opening of a path of revelation, in the theological sense, is to acknowledge something somewhat *beyond* what we normally have in mind when we refer simply to our "environment." Equally, however, the path of revelation is definitely not something bearing no relation to our environment, since the same environment was created through, in, and for the Word, the Son, the *Logos*. Furthermore, the environment in question inevitably acts as a "lens" with respect to our reception of the Word, since it is an environment that has strongly shaped who we are and how we pay attention. Advent is a time to reflect afresh on the place of revelation, in both senses of the word "place"—place as *situated arena* and place as *significant role*. It is a season in which to approach foundational theological ideas through eyes willing to be *opened further* at the start of the liturgical year.

Clearly an absolute prerequisite for being receptive to revelation is first and foremost to be *living*. Living systems are, basically by definition, *open* systems. They can only operate and survive in a sustainable and dynamically stable manner by constantly exchanging various molecules, and various forms of energy and

1. All references to the wording of the Greek text are from Aland et al., *Novum Testamentum Graece*.

information, with their external environment. Admittedly the exchange in question is highly selective and regulated, but even as regulated it is still *open* to the environment. Furthermore, living systems must continually renew and regenerate various parts of themselves. They cannot stay still, but must always be in motion, in process, especially at the molecular scale. Likewise, they are usually developing or changing in some respect, even if in some cases very subtly and not immediately discernibly.

Considering this as something of an analogy for a living journey of discipleship in theological terms, moving further *forward* on our journey is, in this sense, not really an "optional" matter. For a way to be *consistently* opened up for us suggests that our act of moving forward in this way evokes awareness of further opening. In John's Gospel in particular Christ is emphasized as the one who both comes before us but also consistently goes ahead of us, preparing the way. The word "disciple" means the one who learns, and we all know that one of the most notable things about a process of learning is that as new concepts are made open and accessible to us the ground is being laid for yet other concepts to follow. That is why education systems are structured according to the stages that they are, with the potential opening of material that is yet to follow being established through the learning achieved in previous years. A theological journey is *no exception* to this common principle.

As we get older, of course, we do sometimes run the risk of thinking we have learned all the really important things there are to know, but this is foolish, not least because if we do not know *what* it is that we do not yet know then how are we able to judge its relative importance? This seems to me to be the resounding ethos behind Christ telling his disciples that they ultimately have only *one* teacher or instructor (Matt 23:8, 10). Even if we can become teachers *relative to one another*, usually depending on age or level of expertise in a particular subject, and even though other parts of the New Testament suggest that we "ought to be teachers" (Heb 5:12), our continual need to further our own learning, our *progressively opening* journey of discipleship, must not be forgotten or neglected. We must be open to exploring yet further.

If we sometimes get bored with things because they seem the "same old, same old," then we need either to find a way of approaching them through fresh eyes or to resolve to explore some aspect of life or faith, ideally both, that we haven't properly engaged with before. We should remember the biblical saying about the "scribe who has been trained for the kingdom of heaven" being "like the master of a household who brings out of his treasure what is new and what is old" (Matt 13:52). The new does not necessarily contradict the old, it may simply involve the capacity to see the old in a new light, or specifically to build upon it. We are called to seek what is new as well as to guard that which forms our heritage. We are to remain attentive to seeking the indications of the new creation brought into our midst through Christ's death, resurrection, and ascension, while still acknowledging that which has already unfolded in the history of the faith and in the life of the church. This follows the Advent principle of remaining alert, and alert to what may not previously have been anticipated in the run-of-the-mill of what we are routinely accustomed to saying, doing, and repeating in our daily lives. This leads us to the next theme—expecting, anticipating, and awaiting.

Reflection 3

Expecting, Anticipating, Awaiting

There is an important difference between describing someone as waiting and describing them as *a*waiting. The former suggests a significant degree of passivity, and perhaps a very frustrated passivity at that. The latter suggests active anticipation and something that carries a certain sense of momentum into the future. This is a description that puts me in mind of Simoen, eagerly "looking forward to the consolation of Israel" when he receives Jesus in the temple in Luke 2:25–35.

Clearly the big difference between merely waiting and actively awaiting is that in the latter case there is some good reason to expect that something transformative will happen, and perhaps within a particular timeframe. We are not thinking that something might actually never happen. We are not saying to ourselves, "I'll believe that when I see it!" Such active, expectant anticipation will much more likely mean that something constructive is being done *now* in accordance with, and in preparation for, what is being anticipated. Something can be sown now, prepared now, that will have a particular future effect, complementing that which is anticipated when it arrives. This is very different from asking "how long must we wait?", though there will be times when it is inevitable that we might feel this way.

In the Greek version of the New Testament there is a specific form of the past tense that is used when an action in the past continues to exercise its effect in the present, and this is very much the sort of thing we should think of when we note the effect of an enduring, active expectancy and anticipation that has been sown among us. Contained within this is also the idea that you reap what you sow.

Expectancy can be negative of course, and pessimistic expectancy can lead not just to passivity—"well, *I* can do nothing about it"—but also to actively damaging decisions being made that will have further detrimental effects. Living as an *awaiting* people involves carrying a consistent momentum whenever possible, something sufficiently stable in its attitude that, even though there will inevitably be moments where individuals temporarily lose their concentration, their eagerness, or their keenness of hope, enough people are still able to carry the momentum for it to endure. This emphasizes a collective dimension to our Advent-shaped journey together. Enough people need, at any one time, to be able to support others and to bring people back to where they too can *positively* be alert, and prepare and anticipate *now* for the common good.

The parable of the wise and foolish bridesmaids in Matthew 25:1–13 seems at root to be about forward-planning. All the bridesmaids in the parable know that a significant event is to be expected, that a bridegroom is coming whom they need to greet. They know that the call will come to say that the bridegroom's arrival is imminent, but it eventually does so in the thick of night. Five of the bridesmaids have wisely taken a supply of oil with them and five have not. The five who have not done so ask the five who have to share their oil, but are refused because the other five fear that they will not then have enough. They tell the foolish bridesmaids to go and buy oil from those who can supply it, and while they are doing this the bridegroom arrives, enters the wedding banquet with the five wise bridesmaids and shuts the door. When the other bridesmaids arrive at the door, they are told he does not know them, and the parable ends with the classic Advent warning, "Keep awake therefore, for you know neither the day nor the hour," already noted in a previous reflection.

This parable is told in an area of the world of very varied and undulating topography, and also at a time without the benefits of modern technology. Going out after dark without sufficient resource for lighting would have been a potentially very dangerous activity. In the face of unknown timing those concerned would, first of all, have needed to think about how much oil was necessary as a precaution. Later on in the story there is then a second question, namely, whether this precautionary resourcing extends to helping *others* out, or whether they will need to make their own arrangements. Whether sufficient funds or resources are available might also be a question, so in effect we could, in application to a broader context, see a challenge posed here that is socio-political, economic, and logistical. In the story in question the context amounts to knowing ones needs (individually and collectively), knowing your landscape (literally in one sense, but also metaphorically in terms of how we might relate to this parable in our context today), and knowing your uncertainties (not least in terms of timing and duration).

Considered as a metaphor for a way of living more generally, this parable does capture a significant question about our planning, our alertness, and our cooperation. Each generation is faced afresh with these questions, even, if not *especially*, in the face of increasing technological capacity and global-scale interactions. What seems at first a very simple story can, when interpreted as an exhortation to stay awake in any number of *different* possible contexts, so easily take on additional dimensions.

Knowing *what* is anticipated is not the whole story, and, as already stated, all the bridesmaids knew what was afoot but took different attitudes towards it. It is interesting in this sense that the five foolish bridesmaids are told that the bridegroom does not "know" them. If we only know or attend to the "what," at the expense of the how, the when, and perhaps just as importantly the why—concerning our attitude and approach to what is anticipated—then our knowing is not really fully or properly engaged. It doesn't carry the appropriate *momentum* mentioned earlier, and the awaiting is not kept active but disintegrates into mere waiting.

That is not to say that patience is not a virtue, but patience is also very much something that can be kept active, even if it may take on different expressions over the course of time. This also highlights the difference between mood and attitude: our mood invariably changes from one context to another, and often specifically needs to be adjusted to the demands of a given situation—somber or jovial for instance—but attitude can be something more consistent over time, especially if it is an attitude fueled by a continuing sense of expectancy.

The need for activeness and alertness cannot be placed on the shoulders of just one individual of course, except for when the emphasis is on the utterly unique role played by Christ in the reconciliation of creation. From our point of view as disciples, no matter how much motivation we may find in the idea of running a race meaning to win, as Paul puts it in 1 Corinthians 9:24, we do not proclaim a faith where only one competitor in the race can ultimately succeed. Paul's advice is much more a question of attitude, backed up by his reminder, in the very next verse, that those participating properly in the race "exercise self-control in all things." A key aspect of our discipline is in recognizing the *shared* nature of our journey, our race, and our reliance on the encouragement and support of others, not least because of the distribution of different gifts among members of the same body, as Paul famously goes on to emphasize in chapters 12 and 13 of the same letter.

This cooperative aspect of journeying has already extended across several generations, and far more than just two thousand years if we consider what was necessary to prepare for the arrival of Christ in the first place, and at the proper time. The concept of time itself therefore takes on a particular *depth* in Advent, and it is now to this topic that the following three reflections will turn.

Reflection 4

Attending to, in, and with Time

At the time of writing I live in Germany, and in the Protestant Church in Germany the final Sunday of the liturgical year is called *Ewigkeitssonntag*—Eternity Sunday. Not only is it the final Sunday of the church year but also the day on which there is a formal remembrance of those who have departed this life (roughly what All Souls' Day is in the Anglican tradition and elsewhere). The placing of such a commemoration both at the very end of the church year and on a Sunday given to the contemplation of eternity is indeed very fitting.

There are several views on the nature of time and its relation to eternity, but one point that is theologically very important is that eternity is not an endless extension of time, as may sometimes be *mis*-supposed. Eternity is of a different mode to time, as Thomas Aquinas held. It is *outside* time, while time is in some sense held *within* it.

In *The Oxford Companion to Christian Thought* Gerard Loughlin provides a helpful introduction to the question of time, beginning with a reminder that St Augustine (of Hippo) considered time to be only partially knowable, in the sense that as soon as someone inquired into its true nature—what it really, essentially *was*—one moved beyond what could really be known about it, not least because of the fleetingness of the so-called "present." He goes on to describe Augustine's contribution as emphasizing the limitations of considering time with a finite mind—a mind not only influenced by time but whose available language is also structured and limited by the fact that this is the case. Augustine's understanding of time was therefore as something inseparable from the very question of creation and of created beings, according to which we should consider creation not as being placed within some pre-existing time but rather as being brought into existence together *with* it.[1] On this reckoning time has its source in eternity and, furthermore, we have in the Incarnation the fullest meeting of time and eternity in Christ. Among other things, this has implications for the celebration of the Eucharist, as something that both emphasizes time as a divine gift and understands the presence involved as something coming both from what has been and from what is yet to become, drawing the *whole* significance of time into that eternity which is ever-present in Christ.[2]

I mention this here to give a quick flavor of the depth that ought to be reflected in conceptions of time and eternity. We ought also to remember that *how* we view or attend to something itself influences what we believe we see and how we interpret a given context of encounter. Quantum physics has emphasized for many decades now that the act of making a measurement at the quantum scale influences the result of that measurement. Modern psychology also offers great swathes of examples of how the context in which we view something, or the way in which it is presented, strongly influences the manner in which it is interpreted. There are different aspects according to which we may view time, not least given the fact that our means of interpreting it is inseparable from it. There is also the matter of how our appreciation of time is reflected in the potentials and limitations of our language, especially when we are not specifically "measuring" time as such.

What then is specific about the concept of time to the Advent season, to a time that encourages contemplation both upon the arrival of a specifically expected time and upon a pending and yearned for fulfilment both with and within time? In the first instance it is a perspective check, as it were. It asks to what extent are

1. Loughlin, "Time," 707.

2. Loughlin, "Time," 709.

we staying alert to *how* we are attending? In the second instance, even when we believe we are on the alert, are we alert *to* time, as a form of passage or duration, or are we alert *in* time? In other words, are we alert to our finite, materially transient nature and to the fact that our present freedom is defined *according to* our natural constraints rather than in isolation from them? These are both important senses to recognize, but there is also a third—whether we are alert *with* time. To what degree are we able and/or determined to keep track of what is changing and how it is changing, perhaps also why it is changing, while still maintaining a sense for what is not changing, or even unchangeable?

We might broadly think here of the "signs of the times," which will inevitably be seen differently by people living in different contexts, with different points of reference based on their personal history and on that of the culture with which they associate. Again, we need an Advent sense of togetherness that can only come from sharing perspectives and developing a more disciplined awareness of what it is to journey together. Unlike the more personal discipline generally associated with the journey of Lent, Advent is more about asking how, *amidst* our many personal experiences and points of reference, we might discover *together* something of a shared perspective that ultimately involves many generations, over time and with time.

One of the most famous biblical passages regarding time is Ecclesiastes 3:1–15. This begins with the words, "For everything there is a season, and a time for every matter under heaven" and then lists many aspects of this, such as "a time to seek, and a time to lose; a time to keep, and a time to throw away" (verse 6). As the passage develops it becomes more philosophically and theologically poignant, especially when, in verse 11, we read that what, in the Hebrew, is described by the word *o'lam* has been set in the human heart—which we could also translate as "in the mind," since the heart was the intellectual center in the worldview of the time.[3]

3. All references to the wording of the Hebrew text are from The British and Foreign Bible Society, *The Holy Scriptures of the Old Testament.* Possible meanings of Hebrew words are referenced from Davidson, *The Analytical*

O'lam can be translated in a variety of ways, including "world" and "eternity." One way of reading the verse in question translates it as saying that, because the *world* has been set in the human heart, they cannot know what *God* does "from the beginning to the end." An alternative reading shows forth if we translate *o'lam* as eternity, namely, that *even though some sense* of eternity has been set in the heart or mind, at least in a capacity to ponder its nature, there is still that which only God can see or know regarding the relation of beginning to end. The possible ambiguity is compounded by the danger that the phrase "from the beginning to the end" is likely to get read merely as a linear timeline by a modern reader. The Hebrew word used for "beginning" in the opening verse of Genesis, *Reshit*, can also be translated in different ways. It is derived, in turn, from another word meaning very broadly "head," in the sense of that which leads or comes first, something principal or even foundational, such that the idea of beginning could here just as well be understood in terms of foundational principle, or "principal principle" if you prefer a fairly memorable combination of English words.

This clearly has a more dynamic feel to it than conceiving beginning as a static and fairly abstract "point." Indeed, I suspect that, at the very least, the word "place" might convey a more helpful notion here than that of "point," whether or not such is considered as being *within* time. This principle is then duly expanded upon in Ecclesiastes 3:14, when it is stated that "whatever God does endures for ever; nothing can be added to it, nor anything taken from it." The section then ends in the following verse, when we hear that whatever *is* has in some manner *already been* and that whatever is yet to be in some sense "already is." What is *placed* according to the purpose of God is foundational and will be *sought out* as the course of time unfolds. There is something simultaneously comforting and challenging about this idea, and the principle of seeking out speaks to us as an Advent people because it asks us whether we can discern that which is being sought. Can we be properly attentive *to*, *in*, and *with* time as contingent and bounded creatures

---

Hebrew and Chaldee Lexicon.

who have nonetheless been afforded the capacity of glimpsing and pondering the deeper concept of eternity?

If the final Sunday of the church year in many German churches focuses on our conception of eternity, and a sense of shared hope being connected with it, then from the following Sunday, the first Sunday of the new church year in Advent, it is especially fitting to reconsider afresh the nature of time. In particular, we can think of time as coming forth out of that eternity and even as being taken back up into it, through and in the Incarnation which Advent, as *properly attended to*, should prepare us to contemplate with renewed vision.

Reflection 5

Remembering Together

Advent is a season that draws us simultaneously to reflect on past and future. Put slightly differently, its viewpoint is both retrospective and prospective. It is retrospective inasmuch as it reconsiders the depth of history involved in the journey to the moment of Incarnation, encompassing the collective yearning and expectancy that this involved, even if the *form* of the coming in question was *not* exactly what people at the time expected. It is prospective inasmuch as it is aware that there is another form of coming that is still to be expected, or at any rate yet to be completed—what theologians call the eschatological dimension to Advent, which will be the subject of a subsequent reflection. This reflection, however, will focus on a key aspect of the *retrospective* dimension to Advent, namely, from our perspective, memory.

I am interested here particularly in the idea of a collective aspect to memory and to what is involved not simply in an *act* of remembrance but even more importantly in a *process of re-membering*. I use the word "in-volved" deliberately here because, in terms of its etymological roots, it indicates a turning or orienting, or indeed a *re*-orienting, through something occurring *in*wardly. A former Dean of Westminster Abbey, Michael Mayne, pointed out that, while most people probably understand the concept of remembering simply in contrast to forgetting, it could equally well be expressed as re-membering and considered in contrast to dis-membering.[1] Rather than pulling a body or group or community apart it is connected with a process of bringing and holding together, even in the face of conflict. I have cited Mayne on Remembrance Sunday before now, but the application of the point he makes is by no means exclusive to that context. Any communal striving to find some more helpful means of remembering can always in some sense contribute to an *ongoing* process of re-membering and re-conciling the body of an entire community.

Of course, Advent looks to the coming of the one in whose body we can all have a corporate share, in which we are re-membered and reconciled through God's initiative in Christ—something so powerful that we cannot simply refer to the result as a community but rather as a *communion*. That is *not* to say, however, that there is nothing we can do in response, that there is nothing we can do to aid the process of the pursuit of communal good and peace on earth, even if the peace that God gives us in Christ is not *of* this world (John 14:27) and "surpasses all understanding" (Phil 4:7). In order to strive to do so most reasonably and responsibly, however, we need to be alert to the complex nature of human memory.

There are a significant number of different types of memory, largely based upon whether they are long-term or short-term, whether or not they are connected with a habitually familiar procedure, usually involving what we commonly call muscle memory, and whether they are connected with a specific event (episodic memory) or with some fact or knowledge that is not specific to a particular event (semantic memory). There are many finer distinctions, of course, and equally many ways in which memory can be impaired or even simply shown to be unreliable. It is well-known from modern psychology that we remember some aspects of our past far better than others, especially those to which a strong emotional significance was, and maybe still is, attached. It is also known that we do not take in and remember as much information as we think we do, or might like to think we could.

1. Mayne, *Pray, Love, Remember*, 128.

A classic experiment by Chabris and Simons, in which people are asked to keep track of how often a ball is being passed between people wearing white shirts, demonstrates that, in focusing their attention on the ball and the relevant players, viewers of the video often completely miss a person in a gorilla costume appearing in full view. A now equally well-known phenomenon is change blindness, in which changes in features not deemed specifically important to a given context of encounter may be totally missed—they are not details that it seems necessary to search for. A classic demonstration involves a person coming up to someone else and engaging them in conversation, focusing attention on a particular topic or question. During the conversation some workmen walk between them carrying an item that momentarily blocks their view of each other. Behind this barrier the person is swapped with one that looks very roughly similar but would easily stand out as different in a number of respects if both they and the person they swapped with were standing next to each other in plain view. Many people, it seems, don't notice the change.

We also know that memory can specifically be *primed.* What gets remembered is heavily dependent upon the *cue* that is given, and therefore the *context* in which people are asked to recall a story or a historical event affects how they do so. Furthermore, the more times we retell a story over time, the more we may drift away from an accurate account of the events as they actually occurred, but we continue to believe in our memory. Stories are also often told for a particular purpose, because they serve an emotional, political, or social function for an individual, community, or nation. Memory is a *process* and one that is constantly being updated, shaped by personal background and intent, and can fairly easily be influenced by the way in which questions are posed or situations are framed. It may require a great deal of energy and alertness to determine to be as objective as we can.

If this is true at an individual level, then we might simply expect greater complexity on a communal level. Equally, however, communal interaction can *correct* for bias and distortion just as much as it can *reinforce* them, again depending on the context of social encounter and on the nature of our involvement with a situation or group. I used the word re-conciling earlier, in relation to Mayne's point about re-membering, and very deliberately so. While Christians acknowledge that the only eternal, completely efficacious reconciliation—that specifically reconciling humanity *to divinity*—is effected by God in Christ, we also know that there are other processes of social, political, and economic reconciliation between human beings in which we will find ourselves needing to play an active role, as mediators, peacemakers, and peacekeepers. This process is re-*conciliar* in the important sense that it involves taking *council* together, and perhaps *new council* based on hindsight, insight, and foresight, offering fresh or updated advice.

It is important that we are open to such sharing of council, not least because nearly everything gets accompanied by some form of *narrative*, whether official or unofficial, and narrative clearly has the capacity to offend, alienate, and divide just as much as it can enlighten, unite, and affirm. *How* we remember, how we discipline our attention to the *process* of remembering, will be just as important, if not even more so, than *what* is remembered. It will certainly have significant effect on the re-membering and reconciling that we may contribute within our communities, and in some cases directly within ourselves.

If our *way* of attending in itself requires a disciplined attention then it is important for us to realize that there are several dimensions to our attending, to how we may strive to remain alert, and to how we may choose to express or narrate such striving to others. Inevitably there will be contrasts and tensions between some of these dimensions, just as being drawn simultaneously in seemingly contrasting directions in time—retrospective and prospective—implies a residual tension within how we imagine and remember as an Advent people. Having already cited a former Dean of Westminster Abbey it is fitting here also to cite a former Archbishop of Canterbury. In a published Advent sermon Rowan Williams begins by emphasizing Advent as a season of emotional contrast in which there is simultaneously a mood of positive, excited expectancy and one of considerable fear concerning the question of whether we are up to enduring the shaking, idol-shattering nature of God's glory.[2] There is clearly a tension here, a certain double-sidedness. It is important to consider, however, that tension can be a means of storing energy, an elastic potential energy as a physicist would call it, and in a metaphorical sense we can ask whether the tension just mentioned can be harnessed to find an energy that, to take another physics-based metaphor, *does useful work*. Might it be harnessed to reform, transform, or reorientate perspective? In particular, this may become an urgent and possibly critical question at those times when tensions, or even matters in general, develop suddenly and unexpectedly, the topic of the next reflection.

2. Williams, *Open to Judgement*, 7.

Reflection 6

Suddenness and Transition

In many areas of science, but in physics especially, you may hear the phrases "critical phenomena" or "phase transitions" being mentioned, or something fairly similar. These terms refer to instances in which the dynamics of some system are such that there is great sensitivity to the values of various controlling parameters. The most common example of such a parameter is temperature, but other examples might be pressure, density, external magnetic field, concentration, and so forth. The uniting factor is that these systems show very sudden and abrupt changes at various key values of such parameters, known as critical points. The most immediately obvious examples would be the freezing/melting and boiling/condensing points of water where an abrupt change of state—gas to liquid and liquid to solid, or vice versa—is seen at a specific value of the controlling parameter in question, in this case temperature. There are many examples of such phenomena in physics and in several other sciences. One interesting question, therefore, is how we might adopt or adapt the idea of critical points and relevant parameters in terms of *theologically* described phenomena? Advent is a particularly good season in which to ask this question, not least because the *Incarnation* is clearly a prime example of a major, theologically relevant transition.

Suddenness is a definite Advent theme. In the first of these reflections I cited the passage from Mark's Gospel about the danger of being found asleep if the Son of Man comes *suddenly*. Moreover, another classic Advent reading is the passage from Malachi 3:1–4 in which we hear the words "the Lord whom you seek will suddenly come to his temple." Those familiar with Handel's *Messiah* will recognize this verse especially, where the soloist in question renders the word "suddenly" with particular drama and vigor. Speaking of this splendid composition, another Advent text familiar from Handel's work is the passage from Haggai 2:6–7, 9 . . .

> For thus says the Lord of hosts: Once again, in a little while, I will shake the heavens and the earth and the sea and the dry land; and I will shake all the nations, so that the treasure of all nations shall come, and I will fill this house with splendour, says the Lord of hosts . . . The latter splendour of this house shall be greater than the former, says the Lord of hosts; and in this place I will give prosperity, says the Lord of hosts.

First of all, returning briefly to what I said previously about God's "coming towards" and "motioning among" us, facilitating a response by which we are drawn to come to God, we may note another reference to the word "come" in this passage. The treasure of all nations will *come* to the Lord's house, to the temple that is to be rebuilt, remembering especially here the explicit identification between the living temple and Christ's body in John 2:19–21.

Secondly, we should note the word "shake," which implies something that starts *suddenly* and is quite dramatic for a certain period of time before, perhaps equally suddenly, calming down again. In Handel's *Messiah* the soloist shakes his voice so dramatically upon singing the word "shake" that it takes him almost a full five seconds to sing just this single word.

To shake something up is often to reconfigure it. If we say that a shake-up is required, we usually mean a sudden enforced realization that leads to an urgent reorganization of the way things are done. To reach for another physics analogy at this point, consider the process known as annealing. In this process a material, usually a metal, can be made more easily workable, in other words less hard and more ductile. The process involves heating the material to a point higher than the temperature at which it would normally melt/crystallize and then holding the temperature steady at that level for a certain time. This is, as it were, the "shake-up." The material is then cooled and recrystallizes, but in a *different configuration* from before. How this reconfiguration occurs is very dependent on the *rates* of heating and cooling involved, and can therefore in this case be engineered with suitable know-how. Ideally this technique can be used to remove unhelpful stress points in the material in question, which would otherwise limit its workability. Shake-ups can be highly effective, on this analogy, and they can also increase overall stability moving forward.

The reader will easily be able to consider several areas of life where some form of sudden but *well-directed* and *knowledgeable* intervention could produce a far more stable and functional system or setup than the one that was there initially. The Haggai text, rather fittingly on this analogy, also talks of a final state of the house in question that is greater than the former. This passage from Haggai is picked up by the author of the Letter to the Hebrews, who declares in Hebrews 12:26–28 . . .

> At that time his voice shook the earth; but now he has promised, 'Yet once more I will shake not only the earth but also the heaven.' This phrase 'Yet once more' indicates the removal of what is shaken—that is, created things—so that what cannot be shaken may remain. Therefore, since we are receiving a kingdom that cannot be shaken, let us give thanks, by which we offer to God an acceptable worship with reverence and awe.

Although I have chosen to use the NRSV throughout these reflections for the sake of consistency, I should point out that I do not find the word "removal" very helpful here. The Greek word used is *metathesis* and basically means a change or transposition of something, in other words moving something over to a new place, position, or configuration.[1] Furthermore, the word used for what is translated above as "created things" is a participle—a

1. References to possible meanings of Greek words are taken from Liddell and Scott, *Greek-English Lexicon*.

form of a verb—and in this case is expressed in a form implying something which has in one sense been completed in the past but nonetheless continues to have a present relevance and effect (or affect). In other words, the fact that these "things" have been created remains something of relevance, and so to be able to speak of a new creation, as the New Testament does, requires not a sense of irrelevance or annihilation of what was made, but rather a *new relevance* revealed in a *new configuring* and a new "placing" of a newly created, transfigured order—in this case, in Christ.

To return to the theme of shaking and suddenness, it is often the *voice* of the Lord that shakes things in the Old Testament. In some cases this occurs explicitly, such as in Psalm 29, in which the voice of the Lord "is over the waters" (verse 3), "breaks the cedars" (verse 5), "flashes forth flames of fire" (verse 7), "shakes the wilderness" (verse 8), and "strips the forest bare" (verse 9). It is then interesting that these phrases are followed by the words "and in his temple all say, 'Glory!'" In other places there is an implication of the shaking caused by the voice. Not only is it through the voice, through speaking, that the creation in Genesis 1 is presented, but the sound of the Lord God walking in the garden in Genesis 3 causes the man and the woman, having realized their nakedness, to hide from the Lord's presence among the trees of the garden (rather ironically given the above words of Psalm 29!). The Lord's voice calls, "Where are you?", which, in relation to the sense of nomadicism occasioned by the infamous realizing of nakedness before the Lord, is quite a shake-up question in itself.

In Acts 4 we also hear that the early disciples, who had been under an official warning for speaking and teaching in the name of Jesus, pray that God may grant them boldness to do what they need to do. Once they have made this prayer "the place in which they were gathered together was shaken; and they were all filled with the Holy Spirit," (verse 31) which in many ways echoes the imagery of the "violent wind" from heaven in Acts 2:2 in the account of the coming of the Holy Spirit on the day of Pentecost. The shaking is therefore also specifically implicated in the revealing of a new creation, a new configuration, and a new stability.

With this in mind, having now fleshed out somewhat the centrality and the dynamic of *time* as an Advent theme, let us now look back, retrospectively, to the preparation for that new coming towards which Advent draws our attention. Following on from the theme of suddenness and transition especially, the first aspect of this preparation that it is appropriate to reflect upon is the somewhat wild figure of John the Baptist.

Reflection 7
John the Baptist

John the Baptist is one of the traditional focus points of the season of Advent. In one sense he is something of a bridge between Old and New Testaments. We hear about his appearing right at the start of Mark's Gospel, quoting as an introduction the famous line from Isaiah 40:3, "A voice cries out: 'In the wilderness prepare the way of the Lord, make straight in the desert a highway for our God.'" John does indeed appear "in the wilderness" (Mark 1:4) and Jesus himself declares John as being the return of the prophet Elijah, moreover in the interestingly phrased form "if you are willing to accept it, he is Elijah who is to come" (Matt 11:14). Just as John appears relatively suddenly, remembering yesterday's reflection, so does Elijah appear rather suddenly in 1 Kings 17. In Malachi 4:5–6, the final two verses of the entire book, we hear the Lord declaring, "Lo, I will send you the prophet Elijah before the great and terrible day of the Lord comes. He will turn the hearts of parents to their children and the hearts of children to their parents." It is declared that this will mean that the Lord will not strike the land, and, from an Advent perspective, it is interesting that we have both retrospective and prospective viewpoints here—children looking to their parents and parents to their children.

In Matthew's Gospel, just after Elijah and Moses have appeared at the scene of Christ's transfiguration, Christ tells his disciples that Elijah has already come again but the people did not recognize him, and "the disciples understood that he was speaking to them about John the Baptist" (Matt 17:9–13). Just as John's Gospel tells us that the world did not recognize the light and the Word in Christ, even though he came to his own (John 1:10–11), so too it did not recognize "the spirit and power of Elijah" (Luke 1:17) in John the Baptist.

Overall, we do not hear that much about Elijah in the Old Testament, certainly not in comparison with Moses. He appears roughly three quarters of the way through 1 Kings, and by the start of 2 Kings we already hear of his handing over to his successor, Elisha—remembering that John the Baptist also needs to hand over to Jesus. Immediately after he first appears Elijah is sent from one place to another as a drought and famine encroaches on the land. He is first fed by ravens at a place called the Wadi Cherith, then by a widow whose son he ends up bringing back to life at a place called Zarephath. In 1 Kings 18 he is then directed to settle, once and for all, a dispute as to whether the people should make sacrifices to the Lord or to a god known as Baal, effectively a weather god. The victory goes to the Lord, and as a result of this Elijah's life is sought and he flees to the wilderness in 1 Kings 19. He sits under an isolated tree and prays for his death, which might remind us of Jonah's reaction when he does not see the result he seems to want concerning God's judgement on Nineveh (Jonah 4:3, 6–8).

Elijah falls asleep and is then visited by an angel who provides him with enough food and water "for forty days and forty nights"—the Hebrew idiom for "a long time"—while he journeys to Mount Horeb, the mountain at which the Book of Deuteronomy states that the Ten Commandments were given to Moses (Deut 4:10; cf. Exod 3:1, being the site of Moses's famous encounter with the Lord in the burning bush, and Exod 17:6, where Moses later strikes the rock to produce water for the people). At Horeb Elijah comes to a cave where he spends the night, and this is the scene of his famous encounter with the Lord who calls him out of the cave to witness the passing of a mighty wind, then an earthquake, and then fire, in *none* of which the Lord is present. There then follows what the well-known hymn *Dear Lord and Father of Mankind* describes as a "still small voice of calm" but which the NRSV very poignantly refers to as "a sound of sheer silence" (1 Kgs 19:12), as if even silence were somehow resounding sharply in the cave's entrance. *This* is when Elijah is moved to recognize the Lord's presence and he is sent back to the wilderness of Damascus to anoint a new king, Jehu, over Israel—an event which does not actually occur until 2 Kings 9—and hand over to Elisha as his successor.

The next explicit mention of him does not occur until 1 Kings 21:17 when he is sent to give a message of pending destruction to King Ahab, who proceeds to repent, and then he is mentioned again in 2 Kings 1, again in a context of being sent to speak against turning to other gods. He is explicitly noted as a "hairy man, with a leather belt around his waist" (2 Kgs 1:8), which is certainly mirrored in the description of John the Baptist in Matthew 3:4 and Mark 1:6. The final major mention occurs with his famous ascension at the river Jordan in 2 Kings 2, where he also parts the waters with his mantle rather like Moses parts the waters of the Red Sea. He ascends in a whirlwind and is therefore noted for the fact that there is never any mention of his death, hence the expectation of his return.

Overall, in comparison with Moses, Elijah's is a relatively sudden arrival and departure. He is clearly presented as a rather wild and stormy character, accustomed to living on the edge. He says precisely what he thinks, or what he believes himself to be drawn to say by the Lord. His name means "my God is the Lord" and he stands exclusively for the worship of the Lord God of Israel. At two points in the narrative, with the mention of Mount Horeb and the parting of the waters, there are clear associations with Moses, with whom he also appears in the synoptic gospels at the scene of Christ's transfiguration (Matt 17:3; Mark 9:4; Luke 9:30).

John the Baptist is likewise a somewhat stormy figure, who certainly says what he thinks, including addressing the Pharisees and Sadducees as a "brood of vipers" (Luke 3:7). Like Eiljah, he spends quite some time "in the wilderness" (Luke 1:80), eating "locusts and wild honey" (Matt 3:4 and Mark 1:6 again). Similarly, he needs to hand over to someone else, and it is interesting to consider the presentation of this handover in the synoptic gospels. To start with, we know from the Gospel of Luke that the conception of Christ in Mary's womb—or at least the announcement of the fact by the angel Gabriel—took place six months after the conception of John (Luke 1:36). John and Christ therefore already appear, as it were, in opposite seasons, and there seems to be a corresponding distinction in their style of ministry. For example, Christ himself asks

> But to what will I compare this generation? It is like children sitting in the market-places and calling to one another, "We played the flute for you, and you did not dance; we wailed, and you did not mourn." For John came neither eating nor drinking, and they say, "He has a demon"; the Son of Man came eating and drinking, and they say, "Look, a glutton and a drunkard, a friend of tax-collectors and sinners!" (Matt 11:16–19; with a similar account in Luke 7:31–34)

As things develop John's "season" needs to move into that of Christ, the one who comes after him and yet "ranks ahead" of him because he also came before him (John 1:30). Later in John's Gospel we also hear John the Baptist declaring explicitly, "He must increase, but I must decrease" (John 3:30), having already indicated that he is not worthy to untie Christ's sandals (John 1:27). John's disciples gradually move over to Jesus and finally, after he has been arrested, John is beheaded in prison (Matt 14:1–12; Mark 6:14–29; cf. Luke 9:9), while Christ becomes the true head, "the head of the body, the church" (Col 1:18). There can scarcely be a more dramatic decrease in order that another may increase, and furthermore John openly says that his joy is fulfilled in the one who comes after him (John 3:28–29). This humility is despite his being "filled with the Holy Spirit" and "even before his birth" (Luke 1:15) and leaping for joy in his mother's womb as Mary approaches shortly after being told that she is to bear in her own womb the Son of God (Luke 1:41, 44).

The links between these narratives are numerous and point to the idea of one season passing into another. Furthermore, Christ also points to the *dramatic, sudden,* and *transitional* nature of this passing over when he declares, "Truly I tell you, among those born of women no one has arisen greater than John the Baptist; yet the least in the kingdom of heaven is greater than he" (Matt 11:11; cf. Luke 7:28). It is as if John were playing the role of Jesus's best man, organizing all sorts of things in advance of the wedding feast, the consummation of Christ's marriage to his bride, the church. His best man "speech," as it were, is then the voice crying for the Lord's path to be prepared and made straight in the wilderness, and a key consideration for Advent is how our individual paths intermingle. How are they drawn together to become congruent with the Lord's path? The insistence of Moses and Elijah that he is the *only* God is certainly a central aspect of this, since we need to come to the point at which we can say *together* with confidence that "this is *our* God" (considering Ps 48:12–14 for instance). This is far more challenging than simply declaring what "*my* God" is like, since that could on principle be done in relative isolation from others. As Israel's overall witness in the Old Testament shows us, it may take some time to reach the point where the true depth of the collective statement can properly be realized.

There will be times at which endurance seems to fade, tensions dominate, and paths and opinions seem to diverge. The wilderness that we acknowledge in Advent is not an easy place to navigate. To behold the necessary landmarks for our orientation towards the Lord's coming requires insightful reception of the Word of God over many generations. Unlike Lent, in which the journey is a fairly personalized pilgrimage from the wilderness to Jerusalem, Advent is more like a collective, prophecy-oriented development of vision, and it is therefore to a development of the themes of repentance, judgement, and prophecy that the following three reflections will now turn.

Reflection 8

Repentance

When many people hear the word "repent" they might possibly think of fire-and-brimstone-style preaching in which a preacher might easily give the impression of accusing a sizeable proportion of those listening in one way or another. Sometimes we might also get the impression from someone that avoiding certain particular sins is the only thing that really matters, to the possible neglect of much else. To say nothing of the great potential for hypocrisy in such an approach, the first thing that needs to be made clear is that the word repent means at root to *re-think*. This is already somewhat ironic, since in some circles the idea of re-thinking, perhaps changing one's mind on something after a conclusion has supposedly been reached, seems in itself to be seen as a sin.

It is perfectly true of course to say that just to speak about re-thinking is *not* in itself sufficient. It is possible for instance that the consequence of re-thinking could mean abandoning something that is actually quite a good idea, principle or practice, and mistakenly adopting one that is in fact rather damaging in its place. Maybe someone is bored, disillusioned, or frustrated with something that, although at root a good thing, is not producing the results that they want to see or that they believe they have been promised. Perhaps the point has been reached at which there is a knee-jerk rebellion against something, or maybe someone is sick of feeling like they are presenting a certain face or image just for the sake of maintaining a particular socio-political position or status quo.

In order for talk of repentance as *responsible re-thinking* to be meaningful it must be accompanied by the question of how we believe that we best judge between right and wrong, or, in the many, more complex, non-black-and-white cases in life, simply "better" or "worse." To many people the first response is to ask, or to declare, what the Bible "says" about the matter in question. That is all very well until there appear to be different "voices" on the same matter at different places in Scripture, or when something could genuinely be interpreted in more than one way, or where there is a serious question over the best translation of the text, to say nothing of the input of other scholarly schools of biblical commentary or criticism. If the answer to that is simply to say that we don't need all this "academic" stuff, or that we mustn't complicate things by thinking that much, or that a "literal" or "plain" reading is always the best, or that studying theology will lead you astray, or indeed any other attempt to stick to one's first or preferred position without in any manner being challenged by the possible need to re-think, or to think more deeply before reaching a conclusion in the first place, then . . . well, I'm sorry . . . that already shows a certain disinterest in the very concept of repentance as re-thinking, and especially as *responsible* re-thinking. This can be a particular pitfall in cases when such re-thinking might not—at least, not at first—seem to suit us or benefit us. It should equally be borne in mind, however, that people's worldviews don't generally change that much that easily.

The other big danger in failing to appreciate repentance as an *ongoing process* of re-thinking, of learning, of orienting, and of delving more deeply, is that it stifles the idea of discipleship as a journey of growth and maturing over time. A disciple is "the one who learns" and *not* the one who gets to a certain point, possibly while still really quite young, and says "well, I now believe I understand everything that really matters, now it's just about getting as many other people as possible to think and do exactly what I think and do." That is almost the antithesis of the *repenting journey* of discipleship.

Equally, of course, there *are* some sacred truths, or even sacred senses of truth, that shouldn't just be abandoned, and the form of re-thinking being reflected on here is much more about enriching than it is about abandoning. I say the *form* of re-thinking, because at this point the *content* of what that re-thinking may come to involve has not yet been determined—at least, not by *us*. If we have determined in advance the content of what will be concluded, then no matter what route we take to get there, the process can scarcely be described as genuine re-thinking. Even the form of the re-thinking should not be totally predetermined, and this is also something that Rowan Williams, in his aforementioned Advent sermon, mentions in passing when he remarks on the obvious predetermination by which the gold of the people is deliberately formed into the image of a calf in Exodus 32 and yet is still somehow greeted with amazement and awe.[1] To commit oneself to a journey of continual repenting is not to throw potentially valuable things away—to throw the baby out with the bathwater, as it were—but it *is* to acknowledge that, no matter how far we believe we have come in the faith, and no matter how powerful the declarations we make in our places of worship might be, or seem to be, we remain flawed creatures, capable of mis-judgement, of complacency, and of mental laziness and oversimplification, to name but a few.

There are many methods of assessing "personality type" available in the modern world. One that has certainly attracted my attention somewhat more than others in the past is called the *Enneagram*, meaning "nine points" because it is an approach acknowledging nine core typologies of personality. The specific details of the types are not important here, but what is relevant is that there is a strong, albeit slightly mysterious spiritual background to the system in question, and it has attracted significant commentary and attention from several writers who openly hold a strong Christian faith. A lot of what has been written on the

1. Williams, *Open to Judgement*, 9.

subject involves a core assumption that is necessary in order for the system, as the *dynamical spiritual exercise* that it is intended to be, to function appropriately. The assumption in question is simply this: that if we do not pay ongoing and vigilant attention to the path and the developing journey of our discipleship then we will *inevitably* start to "fall asleep." In other words, there is something in (fallen) human nature that means that our "natural" tendency is *not* towards vigilance in this sense—vigilance consciously requires an input of energy on our part. To use another physics analogy, it acts against what we might call spiritual or psychological "entropy."

Left *unattentively* to our own devices, we will naturally drift off and, to use a term very often used in the *Enneagram* literature, disintegrate—perhaps more helpfully written as dis-integrate, as suggesting that the integrity of the wholeness of a person lacks or suffers as a result. Conversely, our deepest spiritual treasures are to be dis-covered, unveiled, if we put the required energy into attending vigilantly to a process of integration. This is very much the spirit of what is being reflected on here concerning responsible re-thinking. It is as much a question of an attentive monitoring of the habits and tendencies by which we *direct* our awareness as it is, from time to time, of changing ideas and opinions as part of a process of growth, learning, maturity, and realization.

It is *not*, however, a question of being so malleable that we will end up believing anything, or indeed nothing, and the warning of 2 Timothy 4:3 that "the time is coming when people will not put up with sound doctrine" still *very much stands*. But equally, it is not a question of being imprisoned, whether by induced fear or by sheer stubbornness, in an impoverished and perhaps self-protectively *oversimplified* worldview in which the very possibility of learning anything from outside what has been "officially" accepted by an individual or a group is automatically excluded. There is a necessary Advent *openness* in the ongoing process of repentance, not merely a fragmented set of individual occasions on which, in one way or another, we explicitly "confess" that which we have done or failed to do.

In the first instance our Advent bearing, in the sense of orientation and navigation, involves asking what it is, what it means, to be open to God. That, in turn, comes to involve the question of how *best* to be open to one another. Sometimes re-thinking might additionally take the form of a shake-up, a more obviously dramatic turning point in the way in which we think and engage with the faith, with others, and with the world. Even this, however, still comes with the necessarily accompanying question as to how we are judging whether this change is for the *better*. Much of the time, however, it may simply be a question of committing to a vigilant and attentive process, as an Advent people, of being better *prepared* for endurance, for resilience, and for being more responsibly aware.

Reflection 9

Judgement as Process

When we consider the placing of Advent in the liturgical calendar we might notice just as much what it comes after as what it comes before. The previous church year has finished with the so-called *kingdom* season, beginning on All Saints' Day and containing what we often think of as the season of remembrance. During this period we have All Souls' Day, we commemorate the victims of conflict and violence on Remembrance Sunday, and, on the final Sunday of the liturgical year, we commemorate the victory of Christ over death, specifically as Christ the *King*. Advent therefore follows on, albeit with a sense of newness and distinction, from a season that has already pointed in solemn earnestness towards themes such as the inevitably of death, the fact of conflict, and the matter of judgement. Advent's particular orientation on this, once again, is towards a *fresh* recognition of God's motioning and coming among us, and the dynamic of the process that this involves for our living experience as disciples.

It is often said in ecclesiastical circles that we must remember that judgement is ultimately God's and not ours. While it is hopefully obvious why this is important to remember, especially in the face of directives such as, "Do not judge, so that you may not be judged" (Matt 7:1), it is equally honest to accept that *anything* which we believe that we know, that we feel, or that we interpret, is done in the *way* that it is precisely because we are human. However we perceive something, and whatever it is that we perceive, it is inescapably from a human point of view, filtered as it is through the intricate and complexly structured phenomenon of the human mind. And that mind has an inescapably subjective aspect to it. Put another way, if we are to say any more about divine judgement other than simply that it happens or that "it is what it is"—if we are to think about or contemplate it in any deeper sense—then we are inevitably using *some form of human judgement* in order to do so.

Equally, it is *not* as if we are *not* called to make judgements in any sense of the expression. In terms of making a reasonable and responsible evaluation or estimation on various matters, this is something we will inevitably do day by day, as much for safety and wellbeing as anything else. Judgement as *estimation* or as *considered evaluation* is very different from judgement as divisiveness and certainly very far from condemnation. Moreover, when we talk of *God's* judgement, it is *in*appropriate to default to a position in which we either automatically import a tone of personal condemnation or unwittingly exclude the possibility that divine judgement is any more than a binary state, a black-and-white matter of yes or no, in or out.

There are people who seem to give this impression when they talk about that judgement that is God's, and sometimes one may get the distinct impression that it is actually rather more theirs than God's. This, however, is more insulting to God than anyone or anything else, since it effectively narrows the entire conception of a divine mind to an either-or, yes-or-no, choice-making mechanism, as if it were some glorified algorithm that sorted things or people into unmovable categories. It also risks ignoring the important sense—indeed, the fact—of the Mind of God being of a very distinctive nature from that of the human mind, and certainly not some "upwards projection" of it. The Mind of God is, apart from anything else, that *by* which, and importantly in accordance with the *creativity of* which, occurs the bringing forth of a deeply intriguing and complex creation.

The nub of the distinction between divine and human mindedness is, in practical terms, summed up in the reminder from Isaiah 55:8–9, "For my thoughts are not your thoughts, nor are your ways my ways, says the Lord. For as the heavens are higher than the earth, so are my ways higher than your ways and my thoughts than your thoughts." We should note here that this occurs literally just before the words from Isaiah 55:10–11 already cited in the opening reflection concerning the Word coming from God's mouth which would not return to him empty but would bear fruit. Just as God's freedom is of a distinctive nature to our freedom, so the same is true of his mind and thought. We are not to "make" God in our image. Simultaneously, however, there must be some sense in which the nature and relevance of our being made in God's image can be discerned, and discerned in a manner accessible to human thought and "judgement" in the broadest sense.

In terms of freedom, the classical doctrine is that God's freedom allows for human freedom. It makes "room" for a distinctive form of freedom that is afforded *by* the divine freedom to do so, and in some sense therefore our freedom *participates* in that greater freedom, at the very least in the sense that it participates in accordance with the opening of the "space" for it to do so. Logically, something similar could be said about the divine mind or mindedness, determining to make space for, or to open a way for, the distinctive activity and freedom of a creaturely mind and consciousness. Among other considerations, this is also what allows there to be a basis both for the very possibility and for the actual fact of the Incarnation—there must clearly be *some distinctive nature* that can be assumed by God, in this case a human nature. Again, this is a dimension in which Advent draws us to view the mystery of Christmas afresh.

The mention of the word "higher" in the Isaiah quotation above may remind some readers of the *Advent Prose*, frequently chanted during this season, which is based on Isaiah 45:8, "Shower, O heavens, from above, and let the skies rain down righteousness; let the earth open, that salvation may spring up, and let it cause righteousness to sprout up also; I the Lord have created it." The mention of the opening of the earth is very fitting here, not least poetically. Any human judgement *concerning* judgement—in the sense of making a sober and responsible evaluation or contemplation regarding judgement, rather than "possessing it" in any absolute sense—needs to be couched within this earthly *openness* to what is beyond. Overall, it is an openness that, among other considerations, allows for the Incarnation, which further emphasizes a form of opening ultimately established by God. God's ownership has involved a union with humanity in Christ, making fullest sense of the name given in Jeremiah 23:5–6 to the one who would be raised up as "a righteous Branch" for David, the name in question being "the LORD is our righteousness" (cf. Jer 33:14–16, already quoted in the opening reflection).

We have the capacity both to form judgement and to fear judgement, or contemplatively to consider what form it might take, or what account of ourselves we could give. We can learn that the measure we give is the one that we ourselves will get (Matt 7:2), learn how to balance our impression of others against keeping a sober and vigilant check upon ourselves, to ask what we need to do in order first to remove the log from our own eye (Matt 7:5). Part of growing to maturity is to reach the point at which some form of judgement, according to human perspective, *can* properly and responsibly be made, but equally to appreciate that, in the light of the Incarnation, this is principally afforded by the fact that God took humanity to himself in Christ, not vice versa. This seems to be very much the tone of the words from Matthew 19:28, when Jesus says, "Truly I tell you, at the renewal of all things, when the Son of Man is seated on the throne of his glory, you who have followed me will also sit on twelve thrones, judging the twelve tribes of Israel." The Greek word here translated in the NRSV as "renewal of all things" is *palingenesia*, coming from *palin*, meaning "again," and *genesis*, meaning (of course) "genesis" or "formation." This illuminates the profundity of meaning here.

Human thought processes will naturally continue to range and network across the world, for better or for worse. The big question, and the big challenge, is how to discern those that are suitably proper and responsible, those that are sufficiently *consonant* with the dynamic of a divine motioning towards a "plan for the fullness of time" (Eph 1:10 again). Indeed, might a *divine* judgement on such thoughts or thought processes even come to reincorporate and transform them in the context of that new creation afforded in the Christ who is both divine *and* human? It is *not* that we can see the entirety of what is involved in the "plan," which clearly we can't, and it is equally not for us to determine the manner in which God may creatively transform or transfigure for the better—that is where faith and trust must hold fast. But we are given more than just a hint that *what* it is to approach something from a human standpoint, one that is simultaneously *being judged* in one sense while itself *forming some manner of judgement* in another sense, is actively meaningful for whatever renewal or transformation is yet to unfold among us.

I will finish this reflection on two aspects of biblical witness that, certainly to my mind, complement one another in this respect. Firstly, there are the words of Simeon when he is presented with Christ in the temple—"This child is destined for the falling and the rising [author's note: notably *in that order*] of many in Israel, and to be a sign that will be opposed so that the inner thoughts of many will be revealed" (Luke 2:34–35).[1] Secondly, there is the part of Ephesians 1:10 not quoted above, in which the "plan for the fullness of time" is described as being "to gather up all things" in Christ or, to offer an arguably more powerful translation of the Greek verb in question, to *recapitulate*, to give a new head to all in Christ.[2] This seems deeply to resonate with the mention of the "inner thoughts" in Luke, especially where renewal, reincorporation, and transformation are concerned.

1. The Greek is powerful here, as the word used for "thoughts" is *dialogismoi*, from which we clearly get the word "dialogues"—something which, in English, is far more socially impactful than simply saying "inner monologue." In this respect the entire Greek phrase used in Luke for "the inner thoughts of many" translates most directly as something like "the dialogues coming forth out of many hearts." Within this verse, in the Greek, a subclause is *embedded* regarding the "sword" that Simeon tells Mary "will pierce your own soul too." A certain piercing sharpness will bring about the revealing in question, a sharpness which, for me, also calls to mind the poetic resonance already noted in the mention of the *sheer* silence in the NRSV translation of Elijah's encounter at the mouth of the cave.

2. This translation is advocated, for example, by Donald Nicholl, with the added reflection that truly to represent the *entirety* of something is to give up having one specific and obvious place within it. It is, in this case, to transcend the whole but nonetheless still be immanent to it. Nicholl, *Holiness*, 17.

Reflection 10

Prophecy

One of the things that we often hear read in churches just *after* Advent is the opening verses of the Letter to the Hebrews, when it is set as the epistle reading for Christmas morning. Specifically, Hebrews 1:1–2 opens by declaring, "Long ago God spoke to our ancestors in many and various ways by the prophets, but in these last days he has spoken to us by a Son [or "the Son"], whom he appointed heir of all things, through whom he also created the worlds." In case the reader is baffled by the plural at the end of this verse, the Greek word here translated as "worlds" is *aiōnas*, from which we get the word "aeons," and, in addition to "worlds," the Greek word can be translated as "ages" or refer to more specific periods of duration such as lifetimes or generations, while in some contexts it can also be translated "eternity." Read into that what you will, but however we translate the Greek it is clear that prophetic activity—including a developing tradition leading up to, and pointing towards, Jesus's time—was varied and spanned several generations.

When we think, as Christians, about fulfilment of prophecy we often look to the fulfilment by Christ in the New Testament of that which was prophesied in the Old Testament or the Hebrew Scriptures. We consider aspects of that literature that stand out in some *sharp relief* when seen through a New Testament lens. Quite a few of these will get mentioned during the course of Advent, not least the traditional O Antiphons that will be the subject of later reflections, in which we find various titles, originally given to figures mentioned in the Hebrew Scriptures, that have been adopted specifically as titles for Christ in the church. Christ is the one understood to have enabled the true fulfilment of the meaning of the title in question. As I said, we shall come to these in due course, but for now the point is that both these, and some of the passages we might for example hear read at a carol service—whether Advent carols or Christmas carols—contain many elements in which we will readily recognize and acknowledge the church's proclamation of fulfilment in Christ.

I used the phrase "sharp relief" to describe how these aspects of the Hebrew Scriptures stand out to us. The word relief can refer either to the removing of a burden—such as that of oppression, tragedy of circumstance, or of the consequences of wrongdoing—or it can refer to the topography of a landscape. In both cases there is an implication of *lifting*: in the first case, the lifting of what would otherwise be a weight too heavy to bear; in the second case, the way in which certain features of a landscape rise above others and may often capture attention more vividly in doing so. Both of these meanings are in some way relevant to the concept of prophecy, or a prophetic tradition, since the spirit of prophecy, and the council that may be achieved through its proper acceptance, is primarily intended either to avoid or ultimately to relieve people of insuperable burdens that might otherwise ensue. Equally, key moments of recognition concerning the place and fulfilment of prophecy grab the attention. Not only that, but a commemoration of such fulfilment becomes firmly embedded within a developing tradition, and perhaps very quickly so. It becomes a key landmark in the relief of a people's collective memory.

Very fittingly, one of the things that many of the people who felt moved to produce the prophetic literature in the Hebrew Scriptures were accustomed to in the region in which they lived was a very rich and varied topography, including both mountainous areas and one of the lowest lying areas in the world, around the Sea of Galilee. We can find references to such topography in a great number of biblical texts, often used specifically to enhance the effectiveness of the text, whether referring to a mountain or to a valley. A text commonly encountered in Advent is the one that speaks about mountains being "made low" and valleys being "lifted up" (Isa 40:4)—a grand levelling-out and in one sense an intriguing social prospect. In the context of the passage in question it prepares the way for the following verse in which we hear, "Then the glory of the Lord shall be revealed, and all people shall see it together, for the mouth of the Lord has spoken" (Isa 40:5, and yet another passage famous to those familiar with Handel's *Messiah*).

Such *togetherness*, noting again the Advent theme of the collective, is possible in this case because of this grand levelling-out, offering a clear image of the possibility of a shared perspective. It has a similar tone to that of the opening verses of Letter to the Hebrews, that the many and varied is here drawn together into one—indeed into *the* One in this case. We hear a similar tone in Jeremiah 31:34, looking towards a new covenant, made with a renewed and rebuilt house in a city that shall never be uprooted. In this context we are told that, "No longer shall they teach one another, or say to each other, 'Know the Lord', for they shall all know me, from the least of them to the greatest, says the Lord." In fact, the entire section of Jeremiah from which this verse comes is quoted later in the Letter to the Hebrews (8:8–12).

We should also note, however, that this levelling-out is not simply some indiscriminate obliteration of the rich topography, or of its important symbolic and attention-directing function more generally. That keeps its place too, with both senses of the term *relief* working effectively in tandem. A few verses after the imagery of the reordering of topography in Isaiah 40, specifically in verse 9, we hear the words, "Get you up to a high mountain, O Zion, herald of good tidings; lift up your voice with strength, O Jerusalem, herald of good tidings, lift it up, do not fear; say to the cities of Judah, 'Here is your God!'" One and the same Word maintains the meaningful and engaging topography of the seer's landscape while also drawing things towards that great unity of perspective foretold a few verses earlier—a transformative reordering housed by the mysterious "place" of the Word that the mouth of the LORD has spoken.

Moreover, the bits that stick out the most, that grab our attention in the relief of a landscape, do not do so in isolation from the overall undulation of that landscape, upon which they are necessary for their stability and their support. Even in the less immediately obvious or attention-grabbing places there will be great value to be gleaned. Consider for example the passage from Luke's Gospel in which the risen Christ, who has encountered the disciples on the way to Emmaus, proceeds to open up the scriptures to them and explain all the places at which they point towards him (Luke 24:27, 44–45). When I preach on this passage I usually ask the question as to whether we would notice *all* the places to which Jesus may have drawn the disciples' attention, including the much more subtle ones that may fall below our normal radar, unless we look closely and discerningly. No explicit list of all the references is given, of course, and perhaps it is more powerful for being both a challenge and an invitation to our imagination and insight, especially given the collective hindsight of two thousand years of church life. Threads of prophetic relevance, intertwined within the overall relief of our encounter, may run very deep indeed.

Adrian Hastings points out that the very individual character of an Old Testament prophet stands in a significant contrast to earlier periods in which whole brotherhoods of prophets existed and prophecy was something shared in across an entire gathering, often at a place deemed to be of great religious significance, and could be a somewhat frenzied affair.[1] He offers 1 Samuel 10:9–12 as an example, in which we hear of the newly anointed Saul being sent on a journey by Samuel, on which he is to meet an entire company of prophets and fall "into a prophetic frenzy" among them. The later prophets known to us from the Hebrew Scriptures were, as he notes, called specifically as individuals, often involving great personal risk, and on the background assumption that the earthly authority towards which the prophecy was directed had a moral duty to fear God and therefore to be open to receiving the

1. Hastings, "Prophecy," 568.

prophecy in the right spirit. The fact that this might not always occur made the prophet's life dangerous, although the authenticity of the prophet often showed itself precisely in the absence of any personal gain—and certainly the absence of material gain—for uttering the prophecy in question.[2] At the same time the prophet was genuinely well-informed and always in some sense pointing to a possible future hope.

The prophet as an outsider, not as within an establishment, could have the recognized advantage of a greater clarity of vision, which could lead to collective change, movement, and even to the prophet being held in great esteem, *if* reception of the message was made in the proper spirit. Such "spirit of prophecy" later came to be equated with "the testimony of Jesus" in Revelation 19:10,[3] and is grounded thereby in an example and practice that is much more than simply being outspokenly critical of contemporary institution. *Anyone* can be outspokenly critical, with varying degrees of informativeness, articulacy, accuracy, and credibility, and certainly great variation in the degree of responsibility or humility. Simply to rock up as the voice of an outsider is not in itself sufficient to maintain and uphold the true spirit of prophecy. Not least, some genuinely constructive input is needed. What is to be built up is ultimately more important than what is to be brought down. As Hastings also reminds us, the fact that a prophet or prophecy may speak against an institutional establishment in some respect is definitely *not* to say that it somehow substitutes for it or simply supersedes it.[4]

For the church the sole and ultimate instituter is, of course, Christ, such that "true worshippers will worship the Father in spirit and truth" (John 4:23), and Christ is well-described as all of "Prophet, Priest, and King," as the hymn *How Sweet the Name of Jesus Sounds* famously exclaims. The last of these is acknowledged,

2. Hastings, "Prophecy," 568–69.

3. There is a potential ambiguity in the Greek here, since it could also conceivably be read "the testimony *to* Jesus," in other words as the witness of discipleship.

4. Hastings, "Prophecy," 569.

among other places, on the Feast of Christ the King on the final Sunday of the liturgical year. Advent then picks up especially on the first of these three and reminds us of a spirit of prophecy that can be *both* a personal sense of calling and conviction *and*, very importantly, a collective sharing in an interdependent discipleship among the members of the church, the body of Christ.

Reflection 11

Hope, Here and Beyond

Hope is traditionally a dominant Advent theme. To be fair to the commercial Advent calendar, it does make us take each day as it comes, and part of the discipline of Advent is developing an expectant but nonetheless *patient* hope. This is something that can be re-examined from one day to the next as we progress through our daily lives, but we also need to consider the nature of hope.

In his letter to the Romans, Paul writes that "in hope we are saved. Now hope that is seen is not hope. For who hopes for what is seen? But if we hope for what we do not see, we wait for it with patience" (Rom 8:24–25). Our seeking and discerning needs to be much more than simply a question of what is most immediately perceivable around us. It is always *more* than our present environment, important to us though that is. Equally, this is not to diminish what *is* seen. In the First Letter of John we hear the opening words, "We declare to you what was from the beginning, what we have heard, what we have seen with our eyes, what we have looked at and touched with our hands" (1 John 1:1). Later on in the same letter there is then the challenging statement that "those who do not love a brother or sister whom they have seen, cannot love God whom they have not seen" (1 John 4:20). For yet another dimension on the important effect of having *seen* something, Christ himself tells his disciples that "many prophets and righteous people longed to see what you see, but did not see it, and to hear what you hear, but did not hear it" (Matt 13:17; cf. Luke 10:24).

In the Letter to the Hebrews we even hear of how the many people who provided lasting examples of a life of faith in the Hebrew Scriptures did not end up receiving what was really being promised, "since God had provided something better so that they would not, without us, be made perfect" (Heb 11:39–40). This again provides a collective dimension to the idea of a lasting and developing hope that is central to Advent. A similar idea is expressed in a slightly different and very bold way in the First Letter of Peter, which first declares to those to whom the letter is addressed, "Although you have not seen him, you love him" (1 Pet 1:8) and then proceeds to say

> Concerning this salvation, the prophets who prophesied of the grace that was to be yours made careful search and inquiry . . . It was revealed to them that they were serving not themselves but you, in regard to the things that have now been announced to you through those who brought you good news by the Holy Spirit sent from heaven—things into which angels long to look! (1 Pet 1:10, 12)

Putting all these texts together, it is clear that the concept of expectant and enduring hope, as well as requiring patience and alertness, also requires an attention both to that which is seen and to that which is not seen. It is not an either-or matter. We celebrate Advent as a people who have in one obvious sense "seen" the fulfilment of the coming of God among us in Christ, including his passion, death, resurrection, and ascension. We know the Christmas and Easter stories and we see what many prophets longed to see. Yet Advent also appeals to what we don't yet see. It asks us to seek more deeply and afresh, with newly opened eyes at the start of the liturgical year, to discern more about the manner in which God motions and dwells in our midst, in a way that might *further direct* the overall, collective vision of those awaiting in earnest hope and expectation. As this may happen quite subtly, we need to keep alert to the signs of how things are moving and developing in our midst.

One immediately obvious aspect of this is that we are never in quite the same place—physically, mentally, or spiritually—as we were during Advent last year. The intervening time will have involved experiences and updated memories that will have some effect or other, whether overt or covert, upon how our sense of hope and expectation may develop and even, to a degree, reform. A living sense of hope is dynamic, not static, and involves many dimensions of our being: a steady patience, yet attentive alertness; recognition of that which is directly known or visible, yet also that which requires searching out, that which is at best seen "dimly" as in, or through, some metaphorical mirror or lens (1 Cor 13:12); that which occasions deep joy, yet also that which requires endurance in suffering.

On this note we should now return to Romans 8, to the passage from which the earlier quotation from Paul was taken, with the question "who hopes for what is seen?" This is part of a far wider reflection from Paul which has much to say about suffering and endurance. Beginning at verse 18, Paul considers "that the sufferings of this present time are not worth comparing with the glory about to be revealed to us" and he then describes the "eager longing" of the *waiting creation* (verse 19), which "was subjected to futility, not of its own will but by the will of the one who subjected it, in hope" (verse 20). Here the hope is sourced in and from God, and of course also *God in Christ*. From the subjective perspective of the creation, Paul uses the metaphor of "labour pains" to describe the inward endurance that awaits redemption, including that new aspect of the creation in Christ which already has "the first fruits of the Spirit" (verses 22–23).

Then comes the aforementioned remark about hope, having *already grounded* the comment about what is not seen, or not yet seen, within the broader context of what *is* sensed, *is* yearned for, *is* presently experienced as tension, as suffering, and as the inward pain of perseverance. Attention is directed towards the fuller presence and appreciation of something newly sown among and within creation—ultimately the complete revealing of the new creation. Then, as a following expression of comfort in our hope, Paul reminds us that "the Spirit helps us in our weakness" and "intercedes with sighs too deep for words" because we do not see or know enough to be clear on how *best* to pray (verse 26). A hope ultimately beyond words is reinforced by a form of intercession too deep for words, and let's be honest about how often we listen to intercessions in church and can't help but feel we've heard it all before, perhaps switching to our own thoughts or inwardly yearning for something that neither we nor the intercessor in question can suitably express.

To my mind there is a distinct resonance in this passage between that which shapes us from the outside—whether the context of the wider creation or even our relation to the utter distinctiveness of the divine nature—and that, from *within*, which responds both to how our perspective has *been* shaped and to the degree of freedom we have *actively* to shape it for ourselves. The more the nature of this resonance differs from one person to another, the more it will be the case that the effects we have on the world and each other risk being arbitrary and fragmentary rather than reinforcing an enduring and shared sense of hope. But the Romans passage indicates quite strongly that there is good reason to presume that a deep commonality is to be found, so that the power of the resonance in question may already collectively reflect something of our shared reason for hope.

This inner striving is further echoed in the Second Letter to the Corinthians, which anticipates the "weight" of glory to come—a positive weight in this case, rather than a burden to bear.

> Even though our outer nature is wasting away, our inner nature is being renewed day by day. For this slight momentary affliction is preparing us for an eternal weight of glory beyond all measure, because we look not at what can be seen but at what cannot be seen; for what can be seen is temporary, but what cannot be seen is eternal (2 Cor 4:16–18).

Some people may object that Paul's worldview is highly dualistic, and of course we do, scientifically speaking, now take a rather different view of the physical world than was common back in Paul's day. It is also true that much that wasn't then seen regarding the physicality of the cosmos, and the implications thereof, *is* now seen, at least to a significantly meaningful degree, after two millennia of scientific advancement. That, in turn, has opened our awareness of what is still not seen, certainly not directly, but which *could possibly become so*, at least indirectly, under the right approach.

There is, however, always at least one irreducible center of gravity to our faith and our hope, in theological terms, which is not seen—that which could not *even on principle* be fully known by anyone other than God. I refer to the united whole *that* and *as* God alone can fully and clearly behold, the consummation of the entire idea, the entire "plan" for creation and re-creation. This thought inevitably draws our attention towards another great Advent theme . . . eschatology, the vision of the end or consummation of all things.

Before we reflect on this, however, and on the development of an inward vision, a contemplation of the "inner nature" just referenced from 2 Corinthians 4, we should first briefly consider two other Advent-relevant themes: the Patriarchs and Matriarchs; and the Law.

Reflection 12

The Patriarchs and Matriarchs

Advent traditionally thinks about those family and tribe leaders, the patriarchs and matriarchs, who played an important and indispensable role in the formation of historical narrative and how it came to be presented to subsequent generations. The most famous and most often talked about are of course Abraham, Isaac, and Jacob, along with their wives, although others are also included under this description.[1] These key figures are associated with questions regarding the nature of one's household, kindred, and homeland. What defines these things, their associated practices, and the enduring story they have to tell?

The concepts of building and keeping a house, preserving a household, and establishing an identity as a particular "people of God" are clearly prevalent in the Hebrew Scriptures and equally clearly reinterpreted in the face of the Incarnation in the New Testament. The Greek word for house is *oikos* and it is one of the two Greek words—the other being the Greek word *nomos*, meaning law, custom, or habitual practice—which together form the roots of the modern word *economy*, the etymological sense of which is therefore about the law, custom, or practice associated with the keeping of a house or household. As we shall see in a subsequent reflection, the term "economy" also has a significant theological import to it.

1. For further reference see Cross and Livingstone, *The Oxford Dictionary of the Christian Church*, 1239.

If we consider the stories of the major patriarchs and matriarchs in Genesis, then it is notable how much of these accounts consist in matters pertaining to sense of homeland, and to keeping a household together, including a strong custom of offering hospitality. It is striking here that the first thing asked by the Lord of Abram, the great father-figure of a people who were to become established through the Lord's call, as the very meaning of the name Abram indicates, is to *leave* his country and kindred and to journey to a land that the Lord would show him (Gen 12:1). He dutifully goes but takes with him "his wife Sarai and his brother's son Lot, and all the possessions that they had gathered," along with "persons whom they had acquired in Haran" (Gen 12:5). A whole household therefore sets out. Abram builds altars to the Lord at various places, pitches his tent, has a remarkably good overall outcome in his encounter with Pharaoh—having gone into Egypt to avoid a famine—and ends up "very rich in livestock, in silver, and in gold" (Gen 13:2). Then there is a conundrum: Lot and Abram have too much each to live together in the same region and household strife was developing (Gen 13:5–7). They agree to part and journey in opposite directions, with Abram settling in Canaan (Gen 13:12). Then, having been promised by the Lord all the land as far as he can see, he moves tent to a place called Hebron and builds another altar (Gen 13:14–18). He even leads some of his trained men to rescue Lot from capture by enemy kings and receives a blessing from "King Melchizedek of Salem" as a result, to whom Abram gives "one-tenth of everything" (Gen 14:14–20).

What Abram wants the most, however, is an heir. At first Sarai offers him Hagar, her Egyptian slave-girl, but this later leads to tension between them when Hagar conceives (Gen 16:1–6). Then the Lord makes a covenant with Abram, now to be Abraham, "the ancestor of a multitude of nations" (Gen 17:5). This is the covenant of circumcision. Sarai is also to be called Sarah and is to bear a son even in old age. Abraham responds to the covenant by having all the males in his household circumcised, including Ishmael, the son Hagar had borne him. The next thing we hear is the famous arrival of three mysterious visitors, to whom Abraham and Sarah immediately offer hospitality and in whom Abraham evidently recognizes the Lord. One of the visitors declares to Abraham, "I will surely return to you in due season, and your wife Sarah shall have a son" (Gen 18:10).

It is notable how much of the imagery involved in the narrative up to Isaac's arrival is related to the finding of a dwelling-place, the keeping together of an extending household, and the tensions that this involves. This further involves the capacity to recognize the Lord's calling, the obedience to maintain a covenant, the resolve to offer hospitality and to give of one's possessions, and the courage even to ask some fairly bold questions of the Lord at various points (Gen 15:2–3; 18:23–33). Abraham even passes the test of being willing to sacrifice Isaac to the Lord, though in the end this is not necessary and a ram is accepted in Isaac's place. As a result of this, the promise regarding Abraham's numerous offspring is reinforced (Gen 22:1–18).

Abraham later makes the oldest servant of his house swear that he will not get a wife for Isaac "from the daughters of the Canaanites" but rather from Abraham's own kindred, and yet also without returning Isaac to the land in question but remaining in the land that has been *promised* (Gen 24:2–9). The circumstances of finding a wife for Isaac involve more offering of hospitality and recognition of kindred, and Rebekah, the one chosen for Isaac, is taken by him into his late mother's tent (Gen 24:67), emphasizing again the strength of the household ethos. When Rebekah subsequently conceives, the two infants struggle within her and she is told by the Lord, "Two nations are in your womb" and furthermore that these two shall be in tension with one another, such that "the elder shall serve the younger" (Gen 25:23). Esau dominates the fields as a hunter and "Jacob was a quiet man, living in tents" (Gen 25:27) and there is even a division of love, with Isaac loving Esau and Rebekah loving Jacob (Gen 25:28). Esau then sells his birthright for a portion of stew when he is hungry (Gen 25:29–34) and Isaac has the promise of a blessing on himself and his descendants reinforced by the Lord (Gen 26:2–5). His prosperity increases (Gen 26:12–14) but he must still search for a stable dwelling-place (Gen 26:17–22) and he too pitches his tent and builds an altar (Gen 26:25).

Jacob then proceeds to take Esau's blessing from Isaac (Gen 27:1–29), and he is also told that he "shall not marry one of the Canaanite women" but find a wife among his kindred (Gen 28:1–2). He then has his own encounter with the Lord involving the vision of the ladder or stairway "reaching to heaven," and the Lord repeats again the promise of offspring being blessed (Gen 28:10–15). Jacob takes the stone on which he had laid his head and pours oil on it in commemoration, along with promising to give one-tenth of all that he is given (Gen 28:18–22), like Abraham before him.

There are, of course, many other details in this narrative, and much more follows Jacob's encounter, including ongoing tension with Esau, but eventually reaching a point of reuniting embrace (Gen 33:1–17), and even being given the name Israel, since he has "striven with God and with humans" and has come through in strength (Gen 32:28). There is yet more in the stories surrounding the establishment of the house of David and the building of the house of the Lord. Key associated themes keep recurring, not least because they are related to a fundamental human need to *belong*.

Parts of the story of Abraham, Isaac, and Jacob may seem culturally quite distant now, even containing things that are highly deceitful and do not sound praiseworthy, thinking for instance of the manner in which Jacob cheats Esau of his blessing. In having the form that they do, however, these stories make an important point about the *non-trivial* task involved in the establishment of household, of custom, of stability in one's dwelling, and ultimately of identity as a collective people—a people who will always be yearning or seeking for something. This is no trivial matter and will involve tension, strength of conviction, and endurance. Sometimes convictions may come to be challenged by subsequent generations, and aspects of culture shift and change. A *dynamic stability of relation*, according to a communicable sense of calling, conviction, and identity, is required over the course of the many generations of offspring that will follow. At the center of narrative gravity there lies the stability of a relation with the Lord, both in a recognition of his presence and in an establishment of covenant. That is the strand of tradition for which the patriarchs and matriarchs most obviously stand.

This reflection may seem somewhat matter-of-fact in comparison with the others offered so far, but the place of the patriarchs and matriarchs illustrates how established senses of identity that form the basis for a lasting and developing tradition must begin from the matter-of-fact need to establish a household and a dwelling-place that can in some sense be called home. At the same time, however, we must not blind ourselves to the constant need to move *forwards*, into the ongoing and developing dynamic, since, as Christ himself reminds us in the gospels, "Foxes have holes, and birds of the air have nests; but the Son of Man has nowhere to lay his head" (Matt 8:20; Luke 9:58).

Reflection 13

The Law

The playwright and theological writer Dorothy Sayers once pointed out that the term "law" is, in common usage, employed in at least two very different manners. On the one hand, it can refer to that laid down by human agreement but which can nonetheless be put into effect, changed, or abolished without in any way changing or influencing the *fundamental* nature of physical existence.[1] These laws ascribe connections between events according to formality rather than to direct and unavoidable physical cause. On the other hand, there are those laws, such as the laws of physics, which are somehow intrinsic to how creation is, to the natural tendencies that it involves.[2] Other so-called laws may loosely refer to certain observed tendencies that do not fall specifically into either of these categories, but as a fundamental requirement we must recognize the difference between these two.

There is a very distinctive sense of freedom in each of these cases. In the first case, the freedom is that the laws *can* be adapted, reinterpreted, or differently applied and upheld. In the second case, the nature of the freedom is *defined* by the nature of the universe, which is already in some respect a *result* of that form of freedom, especially considering the sheer length and depth of cosmic history. Sayers therefore considers what happens when we apply a

1. Sayers, *The Mind of the Maker*, 3.
2. Sayers, *The Mind of the Maker*, 4.

similar logic to the basic nature of humanity. What is relatively certain to follow if human nature is *not heeded*, especially in the formulation of laws of a more arbitrary nature? What constitutes the most reasonable and human-nature-aware manner by which systems of rules and laws may most sustainably and realistically be formulated, without becoming so far removed from the reality of what is faced as to become ineffective, unstable, or unenforceable?

Any officially agreed basis of morality must be as congruent as possible with the unalterable fundamentals of how our physical nature actually is, in order to allow for creative and sustainable freedom.[3] Naivety and defiance with respect to an underlying nature can quickly breed catastrophe, and in this sense evokes some natural judgement or consequence of a negative kind. On the other hand, to remain in keeping, as closely as possible, with a sober experience and realization of how nature is, and how it is best worked with, both generally and more specifically in the case of human nature, is potentially to have a means of flourishing for many generations. Sayers is quick to note the resonance of this with the biblical statement that God would visit "the sins of the fathers upon the children unto the third and fourth generation" while he would also show "mercy unto thousands of them that love Him and keep His commandments" (Deut 5:9–10).[4]

In a previous reflection I mentioned the idea of reconciliation as that which is re-conciliar in the sense of needing to take council together, and to take it afresh from one generation to another, as circumstances, knowledge, hindsight, and insight develop. It is crucial to acknowledge together our dependence on the natural scheme of things with regard to how particular courses of action are likely to pan out. The greater the disruption, the more there will be to reconcile, the harder it will be, and probably the longer it will take. In fact, three or four generations is a pretty good estimate of how long a communal memory of some serious transgression might on average endure in a manner that either blocks early attempts at reconciliation or, at the very least, forces them to yield

3. Sayers, *The Mind of the Maker*, 9.

4. Sayers, *The Mind of the Maker*, 12.

more before there can be a deeper sense of moving on. Moreover, given that one disruption tends to provoke another, it is highly likely that the need for reconciliation will pile up more quickly than human response alone, no matter how well-meaning, can realistically act to reestablish a sense of peace, unity, and concord.

It is theologically acknowledged therefore that God alone can effect true and complete reconciliation. Equally, however, how we respond to the call to contribute to the outworking and the unfolding of what God has enabled in Christ must, if it is to be in any lasting sense effective, be inseparable from a recognition that laws and customs have to be based on a discerning and realistic view of the natural scheme of things. Law has to have a foundational ethos undergirding the manner in which rules are laid down. In the case of the biblical giving of the Law, the Torah, this is summed up in the two greatest commandments as Jesus himself advocates in the gospels: to "love the Lord your God with all your heart, and with all your soul, and with all your might" (Deut 6:5); and to "love your neighbour as yourself" (Lev 19:18).

In terms of what has just been said about consonance with *natural law*, it is very logical first to stipulate that the primary love is to be directed towards the one who fashioned the scheme of things and who therefore has the deepest perspective thereon—the one who knows the true roots of the matter and therefore how most realistically to address it. It is then equally logical to add that the second key principle is to acknowledge the reality of a situation by first reflexively applying the possible effects of an action, decision, or tendency to our own perspective as a human being. From this we can therefore consider how others may be likely to feel and react, and try as hard as we can to imagine their viewpoint. This is not as reliable as a divine perspective or insight, of course, not least because people genuinely do react somewhat *differently* even in very similar if not identical situations. As a secondary principle to accompany the primary principle, however, it is both logical and far more likely to issue in the right form of result than not.

Indeed, even apparent exceptions, in which people do not agree or respond in the manner that we imagine that they might, can still quickly be learned from, especially if *their* perspective is taken as seriously as our own. To put it another way, we might ask to what degree, if we are honest with ourselves, we are prepared to have our perspective, or worldview, or approach to forming opinions changed or challenged. If we acknowledge that this extent is probably quite small in many cases, without being so crass as to attempt to ascribe a percentage to it, then that in turn gives us a rough measure of how much we might reasonably expect others to change.

Insights such as these can, should, and do feed into legal structures and systems, at least in terms of how processes are followed and in the manner of enforcement, or the type of penalty imposed in a given situation. For the very concept of law to be at its most effective, to be appreciated as a reliable guide and as affording a reasonable and responsible form of freedom, it must be searched out deeply enough for such to be realistic. Again, some form of *council* must be sought. In Psalm 119:18 we hear the impassioned plea, "Open my eyes, so that I may behold wondrous things out of your law." This section of the Psalm describes someone who lives "as an alien in the land" (verse 19) and is subject to "scorn and contempt" (verse 22) from those who wander away from the LORD's commandments (verse 21). It is these same commandments which the subject in question does not wish to have hidden from him (verse 19 again). There is a clear desire in these words to see and to explore the law more deeply, to understand the reason that it is what it is, how and why it is to be considered wonderful and its fruit properly beheld. It acknowledges that there is something about its place, its basis, its glory that the Psalmist cannot presently or fully behold in practice, but he knows that it must be there if his eyes can only behold afresh even in the midst of his difficulties.

The Torah was indeed to be studied and contemplated, and the results of that contemplation shared with others. It is not to be seen as a static and merely imposed structure, whether one likes it or not, but rather as a way of learning how best to be and of discerning what we might become as a result, especially in terms of a cohesive society and, in theological terms, a communion.

The establishment of ecclesiastical communion is certainly a clear and strong sense in which Christ *fulfils* rather than abolishes the place and concept of the Torah, and also of the prophets, in terms of revealing something of the divine grounding and purposed motivation behind them, emphasizing that something vital and glorious is thereby to be "accomplished" (Matt 5:17–18).

The practical context of reception and application regarding laws and customs will inevitably change over time in some respect. This is not only because our material context is always in motion—adapting to changing circumstances and acknowledgements that cannot simply be ignored—but also because, to express it in terms of the biblical idiom, the first heavens and the first earth are ultimately to pass away in the unfolding and revelation of a new heavens and new earth (Rev 21:1). It is now therefore to the question of the unfolding of the new creation *into* the final consummation, into the total revealing of the true nature of the "plan for the fullness of time" (Eph 1:10 again), that the next reflection will now turn.

Reflection 14

Eschatology, the Fullness of Time and the Completion of Wholeness

Advent is a season for thinking about eschatology, a word deriving from the Greek word *eschatos*, which has a variety of possible translations but generally indicates the last or most remote of something, like stages in the outworking of a plan or process, for example. It can be viewed spatially or temporally, and possible translations could on principle include farthest, uttermost, uppermost, deepest, innermost, last, finally, and so forth. It is sometimes loosely thought of as pertaining to the "hereafter," but this implies a final stage yet to start and it is frequently emphasized that the final stage of the process is something already begun in the new creation through Christ's death and resurrection. This idea could be compared, for example, to the famous account of Jesus turning water into wine at the wedding at Cana (John 2:1–11), not only as an allegory of the new creation but emphasizing his true role as the real bridegroom in so doing. The chief steward, having tasted the wine, expresses surprise to the bridegroom, whom he presumes to be responsible, that the good wine has been kept until *last*, and in the Greek for "kept" we find once again the use of the Greek tense that implies a completed action which continues to have a present effect. The same tense is also used when Jesus utters his final words, "It is finished" on the cross (John 19:30).

Another key point about eschatology being seen in terms of a final stage in a plan or process is that it emphasizes that to place an eschatological lens on reality is *not* fundamentally to divorce the resulting perspective from the rest of time. This is very important, since we would otherwise run the risk of suggesting that anything coming "before" the point of consummation was somehow irrelevant and contributed no enduring meaning. Among other considerations, it is obvious that our *prospective* outlook will always in some way be influenced by our *retrospective* outlook, or even "in-look," since this inevitably involves our past experience, education, and ever self-nuancing memory in some respect—consciously or subconsciously. Sometimes we are more affected by relatively distant history—that which we have, overall, had more time to process and evaluate, perhaps over many generations—and sometimes more so by relatively recent history. In fact, very recent history is more likely to inform our viewpoint and decisions regarding the very near future, while a *deeper* sense of history—something that is more fully considered over time and with the development of hindsight, foresight, and insight—is likely to have a deeper impact on a longer-term sense and anticipation of the future, whether optimistic or pessimistic.

Thinking eschatologically, however, also involves making some distinctions between the different but complementary aspects that need to be considered. We need to think about the sense in which a closure has been achieved, again in terms of some completed past action, and yet also the sense in which there remains an openness, in terms both of an invitation to the wedding feast and of an incorporation of human response and involvement, albeit with a form of initiative *secondary* to that of God. This is further expressed in the biblical and very Advent-relevant injunctions to "stay alert," the exhortation to "work out" our salvation (Phil 2:12), to move onto "solid food" (Heb 5:12–14, 1 Cor 3:1–2), and to ensure that we complete our journey of faith and finish running "the race that is set before us" (Heb 12:1).

Furthermore, there is a distinction to be made between a "personal" sense of eschatology—the question of the ultimate "place" of the individual—and collective eschatology in the sense of an ultimately *shared beholding* and *united perspective*. There is also the question of cosmic eschatology, relating to the nature and form of the new creation as a whole. From a scientific viewpoint especially, there is the question of the form of physicality that any yet-to-be-fully-revealed reality might present. Finally, there is the question of which aspects of any final consummation might be *continuous* with some sense of the reality we perceive at present and which aspects may be discontinuous. When we consider the transition of ice melting into water, for example, the chemical formula H_2O is continuous, but the arrangement of the molecules involved shifts state from solid to liquid, and this is therefore a form of discontinuity. That is not in any respect intended as a direct analogy for eschatological pondering, of course, but merely to give a sense that, on either "side" of a transition, transformation, or perhaps transfiguration in the theological case, there should be expected to be some aspect of continuity and some aspect of discontinuity.

That having been said, let us examine more closely the passage from Ephesians 1 that talks about the "plan for the fullness of time." The plan in question has its roots "before the foundation of the world" (Eph 1:4) and is therefore thoroughly containing and something always intended to be "in Christ," which also highlights an eternal *in-tending* towards the very possibility and actuality of the Incarnation. The "good pleasure of his [the Father's] will" (Eph 1:5) is to adopt us as children through his Son. Both the good pleasure and also the "mystery" of the Father's will have been "made known to us" in "all wisdom and insight" in Christ (Eph 1:8–9). Recalling the many possible translations of *eschatos* given at the start of this reflection, there is already in this case a clear sense of a deeply held, *innermost* will, conviction, and intention towards the plan and its farthest-reaching consummation. Its potential and its grounding are set out before that of the world itself—an eschatological sense in which the last is in some sense mirrored in the first. Yet this is also, ultimately, to be as fully *revealed* as is possible given that the reception of such revelation must be made by creatures of a distinctive nature, other than that of God. In this sense there is also an *outermost* reach.

Then we come to the verse where the "plan for the fullness of time" is mentioned. The Greek is interesting here, not least etymologically. The phrase translated here as "as a plan" is, in the Greek, *eis oikonomian*, which most directly translates as *into an economy* of the fullness of time. Not only does this highlight the depth of time both as a concept and as a medium for the development of a particular form of creation—of what it *is*, once again, for something to be created, sustained, and redeemed with, through, and in time—but it also highlights a theological application of the term "economy."

Theologians talk of the "divine economy" not so much in the sense of economy as consideration of resource, as in the proper and responsible management of an earthly household for example,[1] but more in the etymological sense of the rule or principle according to which a higher sense of house or household is established. We may talk, for example, of the household of faith, and of what holds it together in an enduring manner. Christ likewise refers to his Father's "house" (John 14:2) in which "there are many dwelling-places." The Father's house is also clearly related to the temple, that which is to be fulfilled in and as the body of Christ (John 2:19–21). The *innermost* place in the original temple construction was the holy of holies, in accordance with which creation was held together. In particular, it housed the seat of the one who *spoke* various orders, decrees, and directions—literally the "oracle," and in this case, of course, a divine oracle. It also housed the Ark of the Covenant and, in the Hebrew, the central seating place of the oracle was the *debir*, which comes from the root word *dabar*. This has many possible translations in different contexts but essentially refers to speaking, or to connecting or communicating more generally.

We hear about this oracle, or the seat or dwelling-place of the oracle, in 1 Kings 6:19 for example, which the NRSV translates, rather fittingly in the context of the current reflection, as, "The inner sanctuary he [Solomon] prepared in the *innermost* [my italics]

1. Equally, however, it does *not neglect* the importance of the fact that such resource is created and given by God.

part of the house, to set there the ark of the covenant of the LORD." The speaking aspect of this also echoes God's speaking, naming, and directing of creation into existence in Genesis 1. When things are then fulfilled in Christ in such a manner as to evoke the recognition of a new creation and a new temple, the eschatological aspect is highlighted very potently, as is the fullness of the divine economy and the ordering of the LORD's house among us.

Ephesians 1:10 then describes the plan, or rather the "economy," *into* which the speaking, ordering, and motioning of the innermost intent of the Father is directed, as being "to gather up all things" in Christ. In the Greek this is *anakephalaiōsasthai*, in which the *ana-* prefix indicates the "up" or something directed up-wards, and the *kephal* part indicates the "head," from which we get words such as en*cephalo*gram describing that by which brain activity is recorded. This can therefore also be translated, as noted earlier, as "recapitulated" in Christ, as "the head of the body, the church" (Col 1:18). This neatly extends the idea of something being according to the mind of God, as from "before the foundation of the world," to that which is according to "the mind of Christ" (cf. 1 Cor 2:16) as the head: gathering, holding together, and summing up . . . consummating and transfiguring.

Advent is filled by many different considerations: our recollectable experience; our present sense of recognition and understanding regarding our physical origins and evolving context; and our response to the challenging questions and demands of our day, whether scientific, sociological, economic, philosophical, or theological. All these can play a part in building *our sense* of what an engaged and "open-economy" view of our eschatological expectation involves, while keeping us realistic and alert regarding how that view may be shaped and influenced, whether helpfully or obstructively. It will involve *both* our collectively relatable experience *and* the more particular drawing of our attention, by various seers and prophets, towards a transcendent aspect of our "place," especially as expressed in those particular styles of biblical literature which move to transform the relief of our more immediate encounter, experience, and perspective.

Reflection 15

Forming an Inward Vision

In the hymn *Now, My Tongue, the Mystery Telling*, which is essentially a hymn about the institution of the sacrament of the Eucharist, we hear the wonderful phrase "faith, our outward sense befriending, makes our inward vision clear." I remember being struck particularly by the invitational power of these words right from the moment I first heard them. There is a type of resonance, enhanced by faith, between the manner in which we outwardly perceive and that in which we seek inner wellbeing and clarity.

That is *not*, of course, to advocate just *any* inner vision, something that could potentially be merely misguided, naïve, or oversimplistic, perhaps preferred simply because it doesn't really take much mental engagement. The whole point of a *process of being alert* with our outward sense, especially as an Advent people, coming to be *befriended by a maturing faith* is that it unfolds over a committed journey of learning that lies at the root of the meaning of discipleship. It is not an invitation to a complacent mental laziness, but rather one that promises great fruit for the inner life, even in difficult times. Effort, love, and energy need to be given to this spiritual exercise of finding resonance, through a developing faith, with that which is gleaned from our outward sense.

The passage from 2 Corinthians 4:16–18, mentioned already in a previous reflection, begins with the words, "So we do not lose heart. Even though our outer nature is wasting away, our inner nature is being renewed day by day." This emphasizes both the encouragement involved in not losing heart and also the daily discipline according to which renewal may be *recognized* within us. The inner nature of this may sound self-indulgent to modern western ears, especially in a society in which, very sadly, introversion and introspection are often ignorantly treated with suspicion or even disdain. Let us not be fooled or pressured into falsely believing that to attend with *due vigilance* to one's inner world, inner dialogue, inner nature, is somehow self-indulgent or wrong. It is actually a vital part of spiritual discipline and of our collective calling.

In fact, there is likely to be far more of a *collective* aspect to someone's inner life than might at first be realized or assumed, and it is logical to suppose this to be the case precisely because of the important link made here with the outward sense. Faith is in this case befriending a means of perceiving an environment that, to a very large extent, we *share*, with its common opportunities, challenges, and concerns. I am not, just to be clear, wishing to play down the importance of individual differences here for one moment, especially since, just like with genetic variation, these play an essential role in providing flexible diversity among the population as a whole. Furthermore, some people clearly have to endure much more challenging, pressured, and negative environments than others, and the spiritual strength that can result from many such cases may make those of us who did not have to endure the difficulty in question stand in respectful wonder.

To a hefty extent, however, there are a great number of aspects of our environment, and of our capacity to engage our senses with them, that a large number of people will share in common. Moreover, to communicate with one another and to share various aspects of the faith is a means of aligning certain aspects of our developing inward vision—or perhaps inward *way of seeing* would be a better means of phrasing it in this case. Through such sharing a strong, communal resonance may come to be appreciated in the way of seeing in question. This, among other things, is how people can agree on the fact that a hymn is particularly meaningful to them, and to enjoy singing it together.

The hymn quoted at the start of this reflection is of course talking predominantly about the fact that, although there is a particular outward appearance to the bread and the wine at communion, there is also a means of engaging in faith in such a manner that the inward result involves a much richer and more meaningful perception than would occur if we simply thought we had done nothing but consume a small bit of bread and a sip of wine. The very word "communion" indicates that this experience is something that is being shared. The deeper meaning of the sacrament in question, a sharing in Christ's suffering and death in order also to share in his resurrection, while finding our place in this sharing as an incorporated member of the body of Christ, the new temple, certainly resonates with a wider consideration of outward sense and its being befriended by faith in our lives *together*. The sacrament is indicative of something that is true for the entirety of those lives, and is ultimately to be more fully recognized as our participation in a greater, shared life.

It might be asked whether there is a working definition of what is meant by "inner nature," or, for that matter, human nature more generally, or even what we refer to as "spirituality." Modern attitude wants crisp definitions, but in this case it should be clear that how you formulate a working definition for any one of these will inevitably affect how you do so for another. Part of the exercise is in discovering more about how our senses of each of them are linked together in practice. Whatever else we might consider our inner nature—or any accompanying inward dialogue, narrative, or vision—to consist in, there is one thing of which we should be certain. It is not, and *should not be*, static. It is a developing dynamic, not to be tied down and individually owned, or kept static out of mental sloth or spiritual stubbornness, but something to be recognized and attended to as *accompanying* faith, and faith in communion with one another. Such accompanying is a mark of the aforementioned befriending, and we should note that the word "companion," from the Latin words *cum* and *panis*, means the one with whom we share bread. Given that the sharing of bread has been given a very sacramentally specific meaning in the Christian tradition of the Eucharist, this idea cannot be taken in banal terms as merely some passing occurrence or gesture before we move onto the next stage and forget all about it.

The famous journey of accompaniment on the Emmaus Road, where a couple of the disciples encounter the risen Christ (Luke 24:13–35), involves a new learning, a new way of beholding the world and the scriptures in faith, that will remain with the disciples even when they no longer behold Christ directly. It is notable that when "they came near the village to which they were going" Jesus motions as if he wants to move further on (Luke 24:28). The two disciples urge him to stay, and they then recognize him in the breaking of the bread, but he *vanishes* as soon as they have done so (Luke 24:29–31). His means of accompaniment is not to be tied down on their terms. They must move further ahead *with* him. They journey at once to tell the other disciples, and Jesus appears while they are in the process of discussing the significance of their encounter and says, "Peace be with you" (Luke 24:36). It is I think quite fitting that, in Luke's account, the giving of peace occurs in a context of discussion, of a *search for significance*, in the midst of a certain degree of confusion among the disciples.

It is precisely when the church is engaged, now on a global scale, in discussion over matters that are not as black-and-white as some would like to believe, where different opinions on significance and different means of interpretation are often rife, that the spirit and context of that giving of peace needs to be remembered. The accompaniment of Christ continues but, as is pointed out by Jesus himself in John's Gospel, he does *not* give peace "as the world gives" (John 14:27). We must continue on the journey rather than halt it through worldly means of avoiding tension, difference, and uncertainty. Luke's account even says of the disciples that "in their joy they were disbelieving and still wondering" (Luke 24:41). Jesus then eats a piece of fish in front of them and opens "their minds to understand the scriptures" (Luke 24:42–45). Afterwards, he leads them out and blesses them, while *simultaneously* withdrawing from them as he ascends (Luke 24:50–51). He therefore vanishes from their sight yet again and the need to continue on the journey moves on still further.

The final words in Luke's Gospel are particularly appropriate for the theme of today's reflection, as they describe the disciples as "continually in the temple blessing God" (Luke 24:53). They have "returned to Jerusalem" by this point (Luke 24:52), and the ending words of the gospel implicitly look forward to the New Jerusalem and the new temple in which our daily discipleship and spiritual discipline is continually to be worked out, and in which the inner nature is to be both discovered and renewed as the outwardly befriending journey of faith continues. Considering therefore the power inherent in such inner vigilance and discipline, it is now just the right time to reflect on another key figure in Advent, the Virgin Mary.

Reflection 16

The Virgin Mary

Advent would clearly not be the season of preparation to reencounter the Incarnation that, among other things, it is without at some point focusing on an obvious person without whom the transition into the Christmas season simply would not have happened—at least, not as we now know it. I speak, of course, of the Virgin Mary, often called the Blessed Virgin Mary or, in the Orthodox Church, the *Theotokos*, the God-bearer.

A description of the circumstances of Jesus's birth and childhood takes up the first two chapters of Luke's Gospel, which is also therefore the gospel in which we hear most about Mary. First there is the famous passage in which the angel Gabriel visits Mary, having already previously appeared to Zechariah, father of John the Baptist, in Luke 1:8–20. Immediately we hear that Mary is "much perplexed by his words and *pondered* [my italics] what sort of greeting this might be" (Luke 1:29). Interestingly, Zechariah responds to Gabriel's message to him—that his wife, Elizabeth, will bear him a son even in her old age—by asking how he can *know* that this will be so, as if demanding a sign. As a consequence, he is temporarily rendered unable to speak (Luke 1:18–20). Mary, by contrast, simply asks, "How can this *be* [my italics], since I am a virgin?" (Luke 1:34).

Faith could well be said to be more a *manner of being* than it is a *matter of knowing*, at the very least in the sense that the way of being is a prerequisite for the way of knowing. Mary's "pondering," about which I shall say more in just a moment, doesn't seem to demand anything *in order to* believe, and she endorses this further with the words "let it be with me according to your word" (Luke 1:38). She proceeds to visit Elizabeth, John the Baptist's mother, who declares, "Blessed are you among women" (Luke 1:42), a phrase that Jesus qualifies later on in the same gospel as indicating the fact of her hearing and obediently receiving the word, and indeed in this case even the Word, that was given to her (Luke 11:27–28).

Twice more in Luke we hear about Mary's pondering. We are told that she "treasured" the words that she heard from the shepherds at the manger regarding what an angel had told them about the newborn child, and that she "pondered them in her heart" (Luke 2:19). A little later in the same chapter we hear that Mary and Joseph find the twelve-year-old Jesus in the temple, having first thought they had lost him and having been searching for him for three days. They witness him astounding the teachers with his understanding and are then asked by Jesus himself why they did not know that he must be in his Father's house. It is then said again that Mary "treasured all these things in her heart" (Luke 2:51). A brief look at the Greek words used is interesting here.

In the first instance, at Gabriel's visit, the word translated as "pondered" is *dielogizeto*, a nominalized form of which—*dialogismoi*—is used again in Luke 2:35 in the context of Simeon describing the infant Christ as "a sign that will be opposed so that the inner thoughts [*dialogismoi*] of many will be revealed," as mentioned in a previous reflection. Very fittingly, this occurs in conjunction with him saying specifically to Mary that her soul too would be pierced by the sharpness of what she was encountering, which would eventually be reflected most potently in her witnessing her son's death on the cross. The Greek word used here is clearly that from which we derive the word "dialogue" and this in turn has its root in the word *logos*, among the *many* possible translations of which is "word," and which in the gospels also refers to that which is to be received from God. With respect to Mary specifically, such reception occurs in a strikingly distinctive and transforming manner.

In the second instance, at the manger with the shepherds, the Greek word translated "treasured" is *synetērei*, which most directly translates as "kept together," and the word translated "pondered" is *symballousa*, which most directly translates as "thrown together" but refers here to mental activity in the sense of things being brought together more clearly in the mind. This latter Greek word is also the origin of the English word "symbol." There are two senses of togetherness held in these words, one in the sense of guardianship and the other in the sense of a projection, following a mental trajectory or several related trajectories, towards an indicated goal or *reference point*. Symbols often only become officially recognized as having the reference that they do when they become cultural norms established within the togetherness of a community, and it is fitting in this sense that the setting of these words is a gathering together around the manger, a setting in which things already need holding together, already point towards something that is yet to come, but are still to be guarded until they can come to be understood in the proper way.

In the third instance, in the temple, the Greek word translated "treasured" is *dietērei*, which is a combination of Greek words meaning "through" and "keep," so again implying an extended period of guardianship. The context, moreover, is in this case now a much larger communal setting than the manger scene. These three concepts—dialogue, guardianship, and symbol—all play a significant part in developing the manner in which an entire community, culture, or nation comes to understand and express its sense of identity. The fact that Mary herself is symbolic of the yearning, searching, hope, and active expectancy of an entire nation is very fitting here. She is the one in whom the form of the expectancy, with a significant degree of *un*expectedness on her part, is transformed even into the biological sense of the expression.

We should also note at this point that the word "obedience" derives from the Latin *obedire*, meaning to listen or to pay attention. Obedience is to do with a proper manner of *attending*, and any accompanying inner dialogue that may be kept and treasured and further pondered over time, is as obedient and attentive as it is also *in proper conjunction with* the word being received. In fact, in the case of Mary, in whom the nature of the expectancy becomes biological, I would even use the word *conjugation* rather than merely conjunction. Conjugation has two meanings in English: one is grammatical, in which a verb, the activity-bearing part of a sense-making sentence, is fitted in its form to the context of the sense of the sentence as a whole; the other is biological, referring to that which is involved in the bringing forth of new life. The first of these meanings was already noted in the theological introduction to this book.

In Mary's case the "conjugation" in question is with respect to the Word or the Verb of God's motioning Activity, to return to the central dynamic mentioned from the outset. She is also the one through whose conception a certain specific *sense* can be made of that Word that would not have been the case if the same Word had not become flesh and dwelt among us. She therefore bridges both meanings of the term "conjugate," and in a distinctively *theological* sense which nonetheless brings forth a *biological* birth. For that matter, she also bridges the two meanings of the word "conceive," both in the sense of an obedient, attention-paying reception and conception of that which she received, and in the sense of the biological conception that ensued. She is, quite rightly, often seen as a highly contemplative figure, one in whom the mental and spiritual senses of the word "conception" continue in her guarding and in her pondering well beyond Jesus's birth. It is important to remember that true contemplative attention-paying is an *active* and demanding process, not a weak or passive one. This fact can easily be overlooked in the modern world, a world often respecting only outward evidence of apparently decisive action.

An active form of expectation ought to *be expected* to have a formational, inward effect, albeit that the form it took in the case of Mary specifically was, to put it mildly, something of a surprise, not least of course to Mary herself. There is a beautiful tradition, not mentioned in the Bible but nonetheless alive in the life of the Church and in the iconographic tradition, in which Mary is taken into temple service at a young age and is allotted the role of spinning the purple and scarlet threads that would form the temple curtain guarding the holy of holies, the innermost sanctuary. The symbolism is immense here, since the child to be conceived in her would become the new temple and open up the inner sanctuary as symbolized in the tearing open of the temple curtain "from top to bottom" at the point of Christ's death on the cross (Matt 27:51; Mark 15:38; cf. Luke 23:45). In order for this to occur, of course, the conception of this divine-human child first needed to be woven or spun together and guarded within Mary (cf. Ps 139:13). Hebrews 10:20 explicitly identifies the "curtain" with Christ's "flesh," and there is a wonderful iconic depiction in which Mary is spinning the curtain thread at the point of Gabriel's annunciation to her. While outwardly engaged in this attention-demanding work, inwardly she is to have the flesh of Christ spun in her womb.

Mary's place in scripture is quietly strong, consistent, and always loaded with meaning and significance in the context or encounter in question. Her attitude is obedient, storing up and pondering in her heart with attentive consistency, being present as a key witness at critical moments, and perhaps we might even say something of a stimulus in the case of moving her son to turn water into wine at the wedding at Cana (John 2:3–5). Last but not least, she is there in the upper room at the awaiting of the church's clothing "with power from on high" (Luke 24:49, Acts 1:12–14). Her mention is in one sense very modest, in another sense a life-enhancing example, and she is the one who is moved to declare with exceptional boldness, "My soul magnifies the Lord" (Luke 1:46). Her pivotal place is acknowledged in Advent especially as consisting in a critical reconstituting and refocusing of a collective, nation-defining hope and expectancy. She is an example for us to be duly attentive to key moments and aspects of revelation, whether overt or covert, that *usher* us along the path of discipleship, to use a fittingly wedding-related metaphor. Even if we do not at first *know* precisely what the fullness of the matter involves, or even *how* we can know that it is the case, as Zechariah questioned, let us, after Mary's example, still actively *be* there in order that it may *be to us* in accordance with the Word being made flesh *among us*.

Reflection 17

O Sapientia, O Wisdom

We now come to the O Antiphons, traditional Advent acclamations of various titles ascribed to Christ that we already find in the Hebrew Scriptures. They have been used since the eighth century, traditionally accompanying the *Magnificat* at Evening Prayer, and many different translations have been used over the centuries. They are also the basis of John Neale's rendering of the famous hymn *O Come, O Come, Emmanuel.* The first antiphon is *O Sapientia*, O Wisdom, and the complete antiphon runs as follows . . .

> "O Wisdom, Which camest forth out of the mouth of the Most High,
> and reachest from one end to the other,
> mightily and sweetly ordering all things:
> Come and teach us the way of prudence."[1]
> (cf. Sir 24:3; Wis 8:1; Prov 9:6)

This antiphon is a combination of three scriptural verses, two of which are from the Apocryphal or Deuterocanonical Books. The first is from Sirach 24:3, in which the Wisdom figure declares, "I came forth from the mouth of the Most High." This is not quite the whole verse, which actually ends with the words "and covered the earth like a mist." In the opening verse of the same chapter

1. This, and the other translations of the O Antiphons that follow, is from Neale (1851), *Hymnal Noted—Parts I and II*, 207–209. The text is originally from the Salisbury Antiphonary.

we hear that she "tells of her glory in the midst of her people." A bit later on we hear that she "compassed the vault of heaven and traversed the depths of the abyss" (Sir 24:5), and then hear her declare that "the Creator of all things gave me a command, and my Creator chose the place for my tent" (Sir 24:8). Furthermore, two verses later, she declares, "In the holy tent I ministered before him" (Sir 24:10). There is a lot of creation imagery in these words, and in Proverbs 8 we also hear of the Wisdom figure, whom, "The LORD created . . . at [or "as"] the beginning of his work" (Prov 8:22).[2] This was "before the beginning of the earth" (Prov 8:23) and we also hear Wisdom declare, "When he established the heavens, I was there" (Prov 8:27). Furthermore, she rejoices in the habitation of the world and delights in humanity (Prov 8:31).

In Genesis 1 God famously "speaks" and "sees" creation into existence. The speaking especially is strongly related to the concept of *Logos*, the Second Person of the Trinity, who is *begotten not created*, as the Nicene Creed reminds us. *Logos* and Wisdom are not quite identical in this case, but very close in the manner in which they are presented, with the latter also being inseparable from the former because she would *not be* without the *Logos*. In a manner very similar to, but somewhat distinct from the *Logos*, she relates both to the speaking in Genesis, since she comes forth from the "mouth of the Most High," and also to the seeing, since she was there as the first "created" or established *witness*, as it were. The *Logos* is famously expressed elsewhere as being "with God" and further as even being God (John 1:1). The association between *Logos* and Wisdom needs to be read somewhat between the lines, but I am tempted to suggest that the Wisdom figure is indicative not so much of *what* is seen—in respect of that seen as "good" and "very good" as the Genesis 1 text progresses—but instead has rather more to do with *how* it is seen. There is here a profoundly *adverbial* quality accompanying the verbal nature of God's

2. It should be noted here especially that there are alternative translations for this part of the Hebrew text. For instance, The British and Foreign Bible Society's *The Holy Scriptures of the Old Testament* translates Proverbs 8:22 as "The LORD possessed me in the beginning of his way, before his works of old," and this clearly carries its own nuance and connotation.

creating, remembering what was said in the introduction to these reflections. In order even for God to have a "view" of creation, that view must be contingent upon that creation—*as* that which is to be created—already being in some respect "in the mind" of God. This affords a resonant relationship between God and that which is *not* God but which is nonetheless to be created as distinctive from God and seen as "good" or "very good" by God and in relation to God. Indeed, it is ultimately to be completed and perfected in and through the *Logos* made flesh.

This is very suitable for an Advent reflection because once again it goes to the roots of the dynamic of the Creator-creature relation, and, as we hear in Proverbs, especially the relation with humankind. This in turn links in with the "image" of God in which humanity is fashioned (Gen 1:26–27), again according to the seeing and intending of God. The title "Most High" is not one we hear that often in the Bible, at least not in comparison to certain other names for God. One place where we very famously hear it, however, is at the visit of the angel Gabriel to Mary. Gabriel tells Mary that, "The Holy Spirit will come upon you, and the power of the Most High will overshadow you" (Luke 1:35) and this language of overshadowing may also remind us of the "mist" with which Wisdom is compared in the above verses from Sirach. In fact, her "throne" is also described as being "in a pillar of cloud" (Sir 24:4).

The Greek word translated as "overshadow" in Luke 1:35 is *episkiasei*, and the same root verb is used again in Luke 9:34, at the point of Jesus's transfiguration. Jesus has been speaking with Moses and Elijah, and Peter talks about making three tents, *skēnas* in the Greek, one for each of them. As he is saying this a cloud comes and overshadows them, a voice declares, "This is my Son" (Luke 9:35), and they then find only Jesus present (Luke 9:36). The encounter in the overshadowing cloud, representative of inhabiting a greater or higher tent, is a key moment of *witness* and brings a new and transfigured perspective to bear in relation to the Christ in whom creation is renewed. The cross references of imagery here are thickly entangled and involve both *Logos* and Wisdom.

The second reference in today's antiphon is from Wisdom 8:1, in which we hear that Wisdom "reaches mightily from one end of the earth to the other, and she orders all things well." A little earlier on in the same book she is described as "more mobile than any motion" (Wis 7:24), of particular interest here given the dynamic Advent theme of God's motioning both *of* and *towards* creation. There is a seamless sense of resonance throughout the divine "speaking" both of and with respect to creation. Moreover, Wisdom is described as "a reflection of eternal light, a spotless mirror of the working of God, and an image of his goodness" (Wis 7:26), again presenting a link to the seeing, to the goodness, and to the divine image noted in Genesis 1.

The final part of the antiphon links in with Proverbs 9:6, which, in the NRSV translation, is worded, "Lay aside immaturity [or "simpleness"], and live, and walk in the way of insight." Wisdom, knowledge, and insight are all Advent themes, inseparably involved in approaching together a genuinely shared perspective *on* our hope and expectation, *in* faith and prayer. Wisdom's united sense of witness affords what, ultimately, *all flesh* is intended to be drawn to *see together* regarding the glory of the LORD (Isa 40:5, part of the classic Advent text also famous from Handel's *Messiah*, as noted earlier).

We have seen that Wisdom is associated both with superlative mobility and also with insight. A juxtaposition of such imagery is also found in the Book of Ezekiel, where we hear about "four living creatures" each one of whom has a wheel, such that, "When they moved, they moved in any of the four directions without veering," and "the rims of all four were full of eyes all round" (Ezek 1:5, 15, 17–18). We hear a very similar description later on in Ezekiel in relation to "four wheels" beside four cherubim, and that "their rims, their spokes, their wings, and the wheels . . . were full of eyes all round" (Ezek 10:9, 12). In Revelation 4:6 we also hear of the seer's vision of "four living creatures, full of eyes in front and behind" and, a couple of verses later, "full of eyes all around and inside" (Rev 4:8a). These are the ones who sing, "Holy, holy, holy, the Lord God the Almighty, who was and is and is to come" (Rev

4:8b), in turn reflecting Isaiah 6:1–4, in which the seer beholds "the Lord sitting on a throne" such that "the hem of his robe filled the temple," while attending seraphim call to one another in flight, *in motion*, saying, "Holy, holy, holy is the Lord of hosts; the whole earth is full of his glory." We are then told that the thresholds *shake*—that Advent theme yet again—and that "the house filled with smoke."

In these richly compact visions we find images of profound mobility, fluent motioning, totality of vision both inward and outward, three-hundred-and-sixty-degree insight, the threefold nature of God, and the shaking revelation of his glory on earth. We hear of smoke, like the overshadowing cloud, a common accompanying image to visions involving the coming of God's glory. The hem of the robe filling the temple may also call to mind the image of the temple curtain and its New Testament association with the flesh of Christ, the one in whom the glory is revealed in fleshly terms. Advent imagery, including the shaking considered in a previous reflection, becomes tightly compacted together in these visions.

The Wisdom figure spans from the highest heavens to the farthest reaches of creation, pervading "all things" (Wis 7:24) and is also practically involved with the wellbeing of humankind in whom she delights, to which other sections of Proverbs, Wisdom, and Sirach bear copious witness. So much is drawn together around this figure, this great witnessing companion or consort, as it were, inseparable from the *Logos* in her activity because she is "created" in tandem with the motioning by which all things come into existence through the *Logos*. The sheer breadth, depth, and beauty of the poetic descriptions surrounding Wisdom may be left to speak for themselves, but the title is equally associated with the work of Christ, precisely because of the inseparable association between Word and Wisdom, regardless of any nitty-gritty discussion surrounding the statement that Wisdom is "created"—though different translations are possible—while the Word is "begotten."

Reflection 18

O Adonai, O Lord

"O Lord, and Ruler of the House of Israel,
Who appearedst unto Moses in a flame of fire in the bush,
and gavest unto him the Law in Sinai:
Come and redeem us with a stretched-out arm."

(cf. Exod 3:2; 6:2–6; 24:12)

Adonai is one of several names that are used for God in the Hebrew Scriptures. It is actually probably plural in its form, rather like the word Elohim, which is also used as a name for God. The plural is thought to reflect the majesty of God and we are likely all familiar with the pluralized form of words in Genesis 1:26, "Let us make humankind in our image." In addition to these names a further tradition developed that the Tetragrammaton, literally the four letters, YHWH, which is the most frequent name for God referred to in the Old Testament, was not to be vocalized aloud, and it came to be replaced in many cases by Adonai. One could argue, therefore, that today's reflection covers both of these names, and perhaps even the very act of addressing God *by any name* in a particular way, and of God choosing to self-reveal in accordance with a particular name.

There is a singular form of Adonai, of course, but rarely used of God, one key exception being in the familiar superlative construction "Lord of lords" in Deuteronomy 10:17. The church famously proclaims Christ as King of kings and Lord of lords, and indeed the name as used in the singular carries royal connotations. The kingly aspect of Christ will be the subject of a later antiphon, but for today the theme is more the direct revealing and addressing of God by name, and indeed, by *different* names. These include, in addition to YHWH, Adonai, and Elohim, the aforementioned Most High, or God Most High, having the Hebrew name El Elyon, whose priest is the famous but biblically little-mentioned figure of Melchizedek. Christ is seen in this case as fulfilling the role of the one who is "a priest for ever," not based on earthly lineage but upon eternal bestowal, "according to the order of Melchizedek" (Ps 110:4; cf. Heb 5:5–10, and more on the same subject in Heb 7).

Furthermore, the short name, El, is the most basic root word used to denote God, but usually qualified in some manner either with a second word or as part of a name given to someone *else*, often to signify the purpose it was believed God had in mind for their life. This includes the angels Michael, Gabriel, and Raphael for example. The number of names ending in -el in the Hebrew Scriptures is huge for precisely this reason. So not only is God being named, but the particularity of the divine *relation* to people, individually and collectively, is also being named, and descendants can in turn be named after their ancestors. In fact, part of the transition implied in the arrival of John the Baptist is in the question over his name, since no one in his family is called John and amazement results when Zechariah pronounces that this is indeed to be his name (Luke 1:61–63). The fact that Zechariah has been momentarily muted and has to write the name down gives this decision an additional sense of authority and engraved permanence.

There are some other names for God too, among them the name Shaddai, or El Shaddai, the meaning of which does not seem to be entirely clear or agreed on, and normally rendered as God Almighty. We find this mainly in the Pentateuch—the five books of Moses from Genesis through to Deuteronomy—but also in

Ezekiel and Job. And, while on the subject of the names themselves, we may further note that the name of God famously given by God to Moses in Exodus 3:14 is slightly different in form to the Tetragrammaton, but both are forms of the root verb "to be." This is especially relevant, not least to Advent, if we recall what was said in the theological introduction to this book.

To consider the finer details regarding the names for God in the Hebrew Scriptures is mainly the province of the biblical scholar, of course, but it is fairly clear that, in several cases, different names may indicate texts stemming originally from different sources that seem to have been combined. The texts that we have now may in some cases contain quite a number of layers, as it were, which in many respects adds to the richness encountered within them.

Another reason, however, why it is fitting for there to be several names for God is that, philosophically speaking, we are not then suggesting that God, the Prime Mover or Motioner, the pure and self-sufficient dynamic of Being-in-Itself, is somehow tied down to, or captured by, one name or one description alone. Likewise, we find several titles for Christ, not only in the antiphons but also in other titles such as the Son of God, the Lamb of God, the Son of Man, the Good Shepherd, the Vine, the Way, the Truth, and the Life, to name but a few.

It is almost certainly clear already that the "motioning" that draws the Advent attention is much more than just physical movement, though it might well involve this in certain contexts. It is just as much about mental and spiritual movement, about that which is indicated or pointed towards, whether explicitly or implicitly. Language inevitably plays a sizeable part in articulating this motioning, or our *sense* thereof, and naming is a key part of that process as long as it does not render static, by doing so, something that should still be seen as directed and developing towards a particular purpose or fulfilment.

Life, or living systems, seem to be imbued with some goal-directed drive that gives a strong sense of being purposeful. The technical term indicating the incorporation of the idea of a goal, or an end-directed purpose, is "teleology," from the Greek word *telos* meaning an end, fulfilment, or consummation of something. While this has become deeply controversial in evolutionary biology it has proved notably difficult to remove the idea, to the point at which biologist J. B. S. Haldane famously compared teleology to the biologist's mistress, since she was needed but not publicly acknowledged. In one sense we can see why describing the *roots* of a sense of purpose may prove tricky, precisely because they are so deeply rooted as to be innate. We are carried and motioned by them every bit as much as we might feel, or like to believe, that we are the ones doing the directing.

Moreover, there is not merely *one* sense of goal or purpose, but several combined, forming a composite sense of purposiveness that is complex and multi-dimensional. Different aspects of this will be emphasized in the context of different encounters, relating to differently perceived openings or opportunities. Different things seem more or most important at different stages in life, and even at different times during a single day, and God must be beyond all of these. This is not just because God is not a "thing"—in the sense of some capturable direct object—but also because the self-sufficiency of divine Being is both the source and, in Christ, also the goal of the very capacity for us to be moved and directed. It is essential, however, that the Being in question is *not* somehow deemed to be captured by our finite capacity, even as image-bearing creatures with respect to that Being. The many different names ascribed to God, and to the relation between Creator and creature with respect both to individuals and to an entire group or nation,[1] speak to the many dimensions involved in, and the many aspects made present by, that *motioning* to which we, as an Advent people, are called to be alert.

Inasmuch as we need to find a way *responsibly* to use language in our theological exploration, in our calling, and in our journeying,

1. Isra*el* for instance, noting again the ending of the name, is a name related to an entire nation and also a name related to Jacob's wrestling with the mysterious divine messenger in Genesis 32, in which he is said to have "striven" with both divinity and humanity. There are many dimensions to such striving and correspondingly several different suggestions as to how best to translate the meaning of the name Israel.

we need to be alert to how our use of language develops, especially as it works around and in conjunction with various linguistic "placeholders." Such placeholders are often nouns, *naming* words, that indicate key reference points. These points help with our orientation towards what is being spoken about, certainly, but we need to bear in mind that they reside within a broader conceptual "space" whose curvature, flexibility, and connectedness—to use a mathematical analogy—we are seeking somehow to explore or to ascertain.

In the introduction to his book *The Edge of Words*, Rowan Williams, whose Advent sermon I cited previously, remarks on how our capacity for language use affords us a means of describing certain *regularities* in our outer and inner environments. Such regularities could perhaps best be thought of as stable aspects of flow, association, and tendency that we frequently or habitually encounter in our lives. The key point is that the regularities themselves are rooted in a *complexity* of physical organization and relations that, in itself, does *not have the same form* as that of our language use and exchange, which occurs of course at the social level and with a grammatical structure. In other words, language, on its own level so to speak, *re*-presents an underlying and enveloping reality,[2] the deeper structure of which we are still learning about.

Williams is writing here in the very broadest sense of the idea of representation, as a *re-presentation* of something in some alternative form and/or medium. We *explore through* such re-presentation, and in so doing we continually re-present, develop, and nuance how we perceive, discern, and describe our sense of stabilizing regularity or consistency in the internal and external reality with which we are faced. Overall, Williams's work suggests that it is when this dynamic and developing reality gets to the point at which there is a certain *edge* to the questions raised by our exploration of it—an edge both in the sense of a sharpness and in the sense of being pushed to the fringe of what words can adequately re-present or describe—that more obviously *theological* connections become suggested and established. At this point an

2. Williams, *The Edge of Words*, x-xi.

overarching and less directly visible connectedness is importantly sought, something holding together our perspective with respect to a *whole* that we cannot, in and of ourselves, capture.

Language use, like Advent, is a *shared* enterprise, and one in which the dynamics underlying how and why we name, describe, re-present, and seek in the way that we do are to be acknowledged as being of great importance. In the midst of these dynamics there remains, theologically speaking, the central acknowledgement that we cannot *fully* capture them any more than we can formally or completely define God, who is, instead, the very source according to which all *else* finds its definition within the overall relief and connectedness of reality.

Reflection 19

O Radix Jesse, O Root of Jesse

"O Root of Jesse, Who standest for an ensign of the people,
at Whom Kings shall shut their mouths,
unto Whom the Gentiles shall pray:
Come and deliver us, and tarry not."

(cf. Isa 11:10; 45:14; 52:15; Rom 15:12)

Let us start here by going back to the very beginning of Isaiah 11: "A shoot shall come out from the stock of Jesse, and a branch shall grow out of his roots." This verse is predominantly about ancestry, about roots in a genealogical sense. Its relevance as a title of Christ lies in the New Testament genealogies of Christ given in Matthew and Luke. Matthew leaps straight in from the start with the genealogy in question, poetically setting it out in three clumps of fourteen generations. There is a profound symbolism involved here. First of all, for something to occur three times is a classic biblical theme indicating that it is time really to sit up and take notice. "God is saying something here" might be a suitable way of summing it up. Consider for example when the Lord calls Samuel three times, which alerts the priest Eli to the fact that the Lord really is "calling the boy" (1 Sam 3:8). The groups of fourteen generations might refer to the fact that letters in Hebrew represented numbers, and the three consonants of the name David have numerical values four, six, and four, totaling fourteen. Matthew wants to emphasize Christ as being both "son of David" and "son of Abraham" (Matt 1:1), two staunch figures in Israel's history, and the number fourteen seems to reinforce the Davidic symbolism.[1]

The clumps of generations lead from Abraham to David, with Jesse being the father of David, then there is a clump from David to the Babylonian deportation, the Exile, and then from the Exile until Jesus. Scholars point out that several generations seem to be missing from Matthew's list, so the fact that it is poetic intent seems fairly indisputable. It also goes through Joseph, who was *not* of course Jesus's biological father. For most Christians, of course, the fact that Jesus is Son of God, born of the Virgin Mary, is much more important for their spirituality and faith in general than that there is a link between his mother's husband and the line of David. That is more a question of pointing to historical connectedness and relevance according to the custom and tradition into which Jesus was born—what it meant for the nation.

Matthew also clearly wishes to make Christ's arrival relevant to the experience of both the Exile into Babylon and the Exodus into Egypt, since it is in his account that we hear of the family of Jesus needing to flee into Egypt to escape the rampages of Herod (Matt 2:13–15). This, alongside the fact that Jesus's arrival, circumstances, and actions fulfil many of the things said by former prophets, is a major emphasis in the early chapters of Matthew.

Luke waits until his third chapter to present his genealogy of Jesus, and rather than begin with the forefathers and list who was the father of whom, as Matthew does, Luke does the reverse. He begins with Jesus and then lists whose son each of a succession of ancestors was. Needless to say, several of the names on his list do not appear in Matthew, and vice versa, and he also chooses to go right the way back to Adam, to whom he refers as "son of God" (Luke 3:38).

Given the absence of modern archives, or of computer records and databases, amassing accurate historical information was

1. Allison, "Matthew," 848.

not the form of task that it is now. The key point here of course is Christ's identity as *the* Son of God and the Second Adam, but still presenting the genealogy in a manner which emphasizes the relevance of the material, historical, and cultural context into which Jesus was born. Put another way, we might say that there is a distinctiveness in the means by which the respective divine and human relevance of Christ is sought, and, for that matter, *why* each is sought.

There is more to the title "root of Jesse" than merely genealogy, however, and this can be seen in how Isaiah 11 develops. "The spirit of the LORD shall rest on him, the spirit of wisdom and understanding, the spirit of counsel and might, the spirit of knowledge and the fear of the LORD" (Isa 11:2). This might remind us of the famous words we encounter earlier in Isaiah, that "he is named Wonderful Counsellor, Mighty God, Everlasting Father, Prince of Peace" (Isa 9:6). In Proverbs 9:10 we are told, "The fear of the LORD is the beginning of wisdom, and the knowledge of the Holy One is insight," providing an obvious link between the various attributes listed in Isaiah 11:2. This pivotal figure brings proper, unbiased judgement and true righteousness, and comes as one who "shall strike the earth with the rod of his mouth" (Isa 11:3–4). The dynamic pivots around the act of proper communication.

A little further on we hear that "the root of Jesse shall stand as a signal to the peoples; the nations shall inquire of him, and his dwelling shall be glorious" (11:10). I mentioned previously the words from Haggai 2:7 regarding "the treasure of all nations" coming and filling the house of the LORD as a result of the LORD shaking the nations. In the words from Isaiah 11:4, with the striking being taken in parallel with the shaking, and in the reference to the inquiry of the nations in Isaiah 11:10, we have a related idea that expresses another dimension to this image from Haggai. Both of these insights are fulfilled in the one whose *manner* of coming was to a large degree unexpected and came with significant ripple effects, among other things revealing the inner thoughts of many, noting Luke 2:35 again, and discerning between helpful and unhelpful ways of seeing, hearing, and speaking according to his unbiased teaching and example.

There is a consistent convergence here upon the dynamics of the Advent motioning, drawing attention to the core of attraction at the center of this dynamic that is ultimately to become the fully revealed dwelling-place of Christ. The divine and human aspects to this are distinct, but nonetheless united in the form of the dwelling in question. The symbol of the *root* has specific relevance here to both the divine and the human. In the human case this relates to finding the most meaningful links with history, with a form of human integrity shaped according to the interactive dynamics of a communal sense of identity, purpose, and calling.

The genealogy provides *part* of the symbolic significance involved in this, but simply in *being* a linguistic species there is something highly important about "the symbolic" in general that in itself speaks to what it means to be human. Over the course of time we have become increasingly aware of how the roots of this significance go even further back, incorporating the history of our species more generally and its evolutionary relation to the various processes of life in the biosphere as a whole. Developing *recognition* of this deep relatedness and interconnectedness adds to and reinforces our symbolic appreciation along with our sense of physical history, of the deep contingency involved in our roots, and of the fact that our means of exploring and learning is heavily context-dependent. We have indeed come a long way towards getting *to the roots* of what it is to be human in biological, historical, and socio-cultural terms.

I say root*s* in the plural because the question of biological history is clearly complex and composite in its nature. If we consider, however, the relevance of the *singular root* to the divine aspect involved, then the root in question becomes a foundational *rootedness* in the Life of God, God as Trinity-in-Unity and Unity-in-Trinity, as the fundamental dynamic of Being and the grounding of all existence. It is a rootedness upon which all other roots are contingent, and it is ultimately only in accordance with the sustenance of such rootedness that *any* genealogy may aspire to the significance and meaning that it does. The season of Advent considers the remarkable fact that this fundamental form of rootedness both affords the very existence of all other discernible roots and pervasively motions through them. In so doing such motioning brings forth something through which a new and radical connectedness with our deepest rootedness may truly be encountered, and with eternal consequences.

Reflection 20

O Clavis David, O Key of David

"O Key of David, and Sceptre of the House of Israel,
Thou That openest and no man shutteth,
and shuttest, and no man openeth:
Come, and loose the prisoner from the prison house,
and him that sitteth in darkness, from the shadow of death."

(cf. Isa 22:22; 42:7; Luke 1:79)

In the Isaiah text upon which this antiphon is primarily based we hear of how the Lord God of hosts gives over authority to a man called Eliakim to be "a father to the inhabitants of Jerusalem," and as a sign of this "the key of the house of David" is placed upon him (Isa 22:20–22). The key is clearly a symbol of the capacity both to open up—already an Advent theme addressed in these reflections—and to close off, to guard. It is therefore a two-edged symbol.

The second part of the antiphon then emphasizes a passage *out of* closure and confinement into an openness beyond. Captivity and slavery are famous images in the Hebrew Scriptures, and the bringing forth out of such is an inseparable part of the people's sense of identity, heritage, and commemorative observance. In the Christian tradition the ultimate captivity is to sin and death. The famous reference to "the valley of the shadow of death" in Psalm 23 appears again in the opening chapter of Luke (verse 79) in the context of the *Benedictus*, the words spoken by Zechariah upon regaining his speech once his son is named as John (the Baptist). These words, now a liturgical canticle, begin with, "Blessed be the Lord God of Israel" followed soon afterwards by reference to the raising up of "a mighty saviour for us in the house of his servant David" (Luke 1:68–69).

Historically the figure of David stood for military strength and national stability. Under him the Ark of the Covenant comes to Jerusalem (2 Sam 6) although the temple itself will not be built until the reign of his successor, Solomon. The covenant is a promise of stability as long as it is maintained. In one sense it is closed and guarded, since it is to consist in a sealed promise or agreement and signify a completed act of establishment. In another sense, however, it must be open to those who seek to follow according to its path, and of course to future generations. Both sides of the symbol of the key are therefore involved.

To be a guardian in one sense while being open in another is in many respects a common human experience. In terms of our evolutionary roots it is easy to see why. We must simultaneously be able to discern an environment's suitability for safety and protection, in which a dwelling might reliably and sustainably be established, and also be able to see open opportunity in the wider surroundings for the support and even expansion of livelihood, not to mention being open to friends and allies. Indeed, the *Benedictus* text also speaks about "being rescued from the hands of our enemies" (Luke 1:73).

Christ's teaching does of course challenge and transform the manner in which both captivity and enmity are viewed. Root captivity becomes emphasized as captivity to sin (John 8:34 for example) and "enemies" become seen as those of whom it must be remembered that they too are victims of such captivity, just as we must also acknowledge our own sinfulness. It is not that enmity is no longer in existence, and certainly not that anything or anyone should just have way made for them to take over. Rather, it is a recognition that the roots of the enmity, and of the *distortion* that leads people to do things that establish or provoke enmity, lie in a form of struggle that is genuinely shared by all humanity, albeit with significantly varying degrees of intent, power, expressive capacity, and self-consciousness.

The double-edged nature of that for which the symbol of the key can stand is inseparable from the roots of our material creaturehood. We now recognize such roots to have developed according to a need for survival in conditions that we often simply refer to as "the wild," and we now also know that hunter-gatherer communities spanned the vast proportion of our species' overall history. The time since the adaptation of subsistence agriculture and the establishment of bigger, permanent settlement constitutes a relatively small percentage of this history. In this respect it is especially fitting that John the Baptist "was in the wilderness until the day he appeared publicly to Israel" (Luke 1:80). To more deeply appreciate the nature of the paths that would need preparing, and *how* human nature may take to them, is to be increasingly aware of the historical intensity of our relation to the raw wildness of what we commonly call the natural world. This world is in several respects *more real* than what we sometimes refer to as the "real world"—a phrase that is all too often used in reference to that "world" which human society, language, and commerce has made *for itself* and negotiates among itself, often to the benefit of those with the greatest proportion of power or strength of expression.

Part of the ecological crisis with which we are faced has to do with historical failure rightly to discern, appreciate, and respect those ways in which the natural world needs to be guarded and uninvaded—protected through a *closure* to interference—and those in which it needs to be *open* as resource. Furthermore, to fail to appreciate the *flowing* nature of resource is all too often to set up barriers that block key channels of flow and communication and thereby starve crucial aspects of the natural order, only to realize later the critical part they played in the complex interconnectedness of a wider ecology.

Whether we talk of ways, paths, or flows, we need to be considering how processes of proper relation and communication naturally function best, *such that* they can lay the grounding for a sustainable way forward, a proper recognition of where our errors lie, and a responsible reaction to the eventual inevitability of death in this world. Ours is always a world in tension, so it is a question of acknowledging that tension in a proper and balanced manner, always aiming for better relations with one another, so that the whole ecology may persist in a manner still allowing the light of deeper appreciation, knowledge, and insight to reach even into what might seem like the darkest places of life. That certainly seems to me to be the tone on which the *Benedictus* concludes, not least in its suggestion that this is a way towards finding the meaning of a true peace.

An important aspect of the metaphor of the key also lies in a recognition of why a particular means of relating between various tensions of life may be effective in penetrating beyond the surface appearance of a particular context. *Making* keys is of course a very skilled enterprise and attention to detail is crucial. If a key is to be copied then it must be done with great accuracy, and small deviations could result in dysfunctionality. The same is true for electronic keys and codes more generally. If the detail is not correct then there is no means of opening up, and a tiny change can have a profound effect. Metaphorically, the same is true of an "aha" moment, in which a small shift in the way something is presented can make all the difference in terms of profundity of recognition. This can open up considerable vistas for people, with lifelong and life-enhancing consequences.

When we attribute the notion of the Key of David to Christ, indicating a new house and correspondingly new form of household, we must remember that Christ is not just the keyholder, but also the one who famously promises to give "the keys of the kingdom of heaven" to Peter (Matt 16:19). Furthermore, he is the one *through and in whom* the key to the roots and foundation of creation, to the deeply pervading dynamic of reality itself, is fashioned in all its exactingness, and according to whom a new way is correspondingly opened. Creation has come through him in the first place and his motioning through creation in human flesh draws creation to him afresh, and importantly under an utterly unique perspective that he, and he alone, possesses. The key in question is of a totally unique form, and hence the great sense of particularity and permanence of which today's antiphon speaks, while still holding fast the prayerful confidence that looks towards the loosing of captivity and the victory over death.

Our view of household, of that which holds us together, becomes transformed in Christ, and Advent is at least partly about a re-orientation to this transformed context in Christ. This is a key (no pun intended) aspect of our prospective outlook, and it is therefore fittingly to a theme strongly connected with such re-orientation that we turn with our next antiphon.

Reflection 21

O Oriens, O Orient

"O Orient,
Brightness of the Eternal Light, and Sun of Righteousness:
Come and lighten them that sit in darkness,
and in the shadow of death."

(cf. Mal 4:2; Rev 22:16; Luke 1:78–79)

This antiphon extends the tone expressed toward the end of the *Benedictus* in Luke 1:78–79 to a connection with other parts of Scripture. The "dawn from on high" in verse 78 is now held in relation to the "sun of righteousness," from Malachi 4:2, which "shall rise, with healing in its wings." In the context of Malachi this is in conjunction with "the arrogant and all evildoers" being left with "neither root nor branch" (4:1), which again speaks to the idea of a thorough and fundamental transition and renewal through the dawning which is to occur. The end of the chapter then foretells the sending of Elijah, identified by Christ with John the Baptist, which establishes a further link between this section of Malachi and the *Benedictus*.

Furthermore, the antiphon links in with the Wisdom figure as "a reflection of eternal light" (Wis 7:26 again). In terms of created light, the moon reflects the light of the sun; in terms of uncreated light, as expressed for example in Revelation 21:23 and 22:5—also expressing a vision of the heavenly city, the New Jerusalem—Christ's humanity reflects the light of his divinity. In the vision in Revelation 21 this is something pervading the *entirety* of the reality in question, since no specifically located temple is in evidence within the city (Rev 21:22). Through New Testament eyes, Wisdom could in this sense also be seen as a figure witnessing the *eternal intention* towards the Incarnation, "before the foundation of the world" (Eph 1:4 again), and indicating at least some resonant relation between the eternal light and the "Let there be light" pronouncement of Genesis 1:3. There is perhaps also a hint of this, again as seen through New Testament eyes, in Psalm 110:3, with the mention of "the womb of the morning," or of the dawn, which is placed in parallel with the idea of one who is "a priest for ever according to the order of Melchizedek" (verse 4).

In Revelation 22:16, following on from the description of the heavenly city, we hear a figure explicitly identified as Jesus declaring "I am the root and the descendant of David, the bright morning star," followed in the very next verse by a fittingly Advent invitation to "come"—a word used three times in the same verse. A considerable variety of imagery is drawn together here, and, in relation to the idea of a dawning, we should remember that the dawn in question is to be recognized *at its dawning*. The *eternal* nature of this light means that it is *not* a matter of waiting for noon, as it were, for the light to be properly acknowledged or deemed sufficiently bright or glorious.

The Latin title for the antiphon, *O Oriens*, refers of course to the orient, the east, the direction of dawning. It is also, perhaps equally suitably, the origin of the word "orientation," that according to which a sense of true situatedness and directedness is found and enlightened. In the Old Testament we hear that the Garden of Eden was "in the east" (Gen 2:8) and, after the expulsion of the man and the woman, is also guarded "at the east" by cherubim and a "flaming and turning" sword (Gen 3:24). Likewise, it is clear from Exodus 27:9–16 that it was towards the east that the tabernacle of the LORD faced, since we hear it said only of "the court on the front to the east" (verse 13) that there is to be a gap in the hangings to make way for a gate, with "a screen . . . of blue, purple, and crimson yarns, and of fine twisted linen, embroidered with needlework" (verse 16). The west side is also referred to as "the rear" (Exod 26:22, 27). In 1 Kings 6:23–35 we hear about the positioning of carved images of cherubim around the sanctuary, which are guardian figures, thereby reinforcing a parallel between the temple and the garden. These cherubim figures are also referenced in the temple vision of Ezekiel 41:15–26.

In fact, it is in the Book of Ezekiel that we hear perhaps the greatest emphasis on the special nature of eastward orientation, a tradition continued in a huge number of church buildings to this day. In Ezekiel 11:1 we hear of "the house of the Lord, which faces east" (cf. Ezek 47:1). Then, when the temple area is explored and measured in the vision beginning in chapter 40, the man with "the measuring reed" begins at "the gateway facing east" (40:5–6). Later on, after "measuring the interior of the temple area" he leads the seer out through the east gate (42:15). A few verses later the seer is brought back to the east gate and beholds "the glory of the God of Israel . . . coming from the east," which then enters the temple by the east gate (43:1–2, 4). The beholding of the divine glory is here inseparable from this sense of proper orientation.

The process of dawning, gentle though in many respects it sounds, also contains a sense of Advent suddenness. Even across a flat landscape with a clear view of the horizon there is a tipping point at which a significant quantity of light quite suddenly appears over the horizon in a short time-span. The orientation provided by the symbolism of facing east is, if you like, the "principal axis" of our Advent calling to alertness and vigilance. It is an orientation both of greeting and of anticipation concerning a key and relatively sudden turning point. While symbols themselves can only take us so far, it is the anticipation of having life "abundantly" (John 10:10) that fuels a determination to remain vigilant to the question of proper orientation. The reference from John's Gospel here is, appropriately, that of Christ referring to himself as both "the gate for the sheep" (John 10:7) and the guiding shepherd, and specifically in *contrast* to the thief who breaks in "to steal and kill and destroy" (John 10:10 again).

From a New Testament perspective, the fulfilment of the coming glory of God enters the new temple in Christ. In Hebrew the word for glory, *kabod*, is connected with the idea of having a certain weight or importance, perhaps most helpfully thought of in this context in terms of providing a fundamental and stabilizing *center of gravity*. Such a sense of centeredness affords a reliable grounding for our orientation and simultaneously draws us towards appropriate reverence. In Ezekiel especially, but also elsewhere in the Old Testament, we hear of some very lengthy and meticulous attention paid to measuring the various dimensions and aspects of the temple, something clearly deemed to be highly meaningful since *all* that the seer beheld was to be declared "to the house of Israel" (Ezek 40:4).

In comparison to the previous reflection regarding the key, there is something similarly exacting here in terms of an anticipation of what the temple would need to accommodate. Translated into a living and embodied context by and in Christ, the nature of the exactingness is shown to be profoundly rooted in the dynamic nature of the relation between Creator and creation, and especially between divinity and humanity. A very specific, *incarnational key* is needed to unlock the mystery of, and the path to, the abundance of life that is promised. Advent does not ask us to get to know every detail involved—that would be impossible—but it does ask us to search out something of that renewed orientation which Christ affords us and to explore our involvement in this new temple with increasing breadth and depth. Ultimately, the richness of this new context is as immense as the exacting attentiveness by which it has been prepared for us.

That such attentiveness is unique to the perspective of Christ has already been clearly suggested. In one sense the eternal light is of a brightness that we might appropriately think of as being beyond that which is tolerable by our normal perception—hence its penetrating and pervading nature. We do not in this sense see the detail or exactingness in a clear and focal manner. In one sense this is because, rather than drawing our attention to one part or point within the whole, it is the *whole itself* that is being transformed and refocused. This is certainly mirrored in the imagery from Ezekiel, with its powerful weight of emphasis on the glory of the Lord entering the temple

One key distinction in the new context of orientation in Christ may well be precisely in the nature of the *holding together* of the whole (cf. Col 1:17). There are many senses in which we might think of or imagine this, but one of them will show forth in an understanding of Christ as the Governor or King of the domain or realm in question. This is now the subject of the next antiphon.

Reflection 22

O Rex gentium, O King of the Gentiles

"O King of the Gentiles, and their Desire,
the Cornerstone, Who madest both one:
Come and save man,
whom Thou hast made out of the dust of the earth."
(cf. Jer 10:7; Isa 28:16; Eph 2:14; Gen 2:7)

There is a notable contrast in this antiphon between the relative instability of the "dust," from which humanity is fashioned in the imagery of Genesis 2:7—*a'damah* (dust, land, or soil) in the Hebrew—and the "cornerstone" or "foundation stone" laid in Zion, "a tested stone" and "a sure foundation," in Isaiah 28:16. In Psalm 118:22 there is a further association between this stone and that which "the builders rejected," and in Ephesians 2:20 the cornerstone is explicitly identified with Christ, enabling in turn the proper "foundation of the apostles and prophets." This is just a few verses after the reference to Christ making Jews and Gentiles as one (Eph 2:14), and the following verse then refers to "the whole structure" being "joined together" in Christ such that it "grows into a holy temple in the Lord" (Eph 2:21). The people of this new kingdom—indeed, a new *form* of kingdom—"are built together spiritually ["in the Spirit" in the Greek] into a dwelling-place for

God" (Eph 2:22). Christ is both the new temple and the establisher of a New Eden, and the Second Adam in whom the *of-the-earth* nature of "the man," *a'dam* in the Hebrew, is transformed into something founded not just by God but even upon God—the God who actively assumes human form, a human nature, in order to effect the transformation in question.

The antiphon also carries an obvious monarchic reference. Although monarchy and priesthood are different things, the line of Melchizedek does form a relation between the role of king and priest, but according to a different conception of priesthood from that based on earthly lineage. Moreover, the same Hebrew word, *hekal*, can mean both palace or temple. Christ famously fulfils all the roles of prophet, priest, and king, and the temple concept is one that can form a context of unity for these roles, not least because it is that in accordance with which a community becomes gathered and defined in its theological orientation and liturgical practice—in the broadest sense of word "liturgical," according to its Greek roots, as a work or activity of praise involving an entire people.

In 2 Samuel 8:15 we hear that David, as king "over all Israel," is allotted the role of administering "justice and equity" to the people. One of the Hebrew words used here is *tzedakah*, often translated as "righteousness" but sometimes as justice or equity, and which indicates charitableness in particular. In a book of Lenten reflections, Paul Dominiak helpfully reminds his readers that righteousness means, at root, establishing or reestablishing a proper and appropriate means of relating,[1] and this is important to bear in mind when we emphasize Christ as King. We have already heard in today's antiphon about Christ making "both one," but there is even more to it than that, of course, because there is also the matter of *individual* differences rather than simply those between groups. These differences lie at the root of much of the ongoing need for reconciliation, even among those who would identify as being church members according to the same tradition or denomination. This search for unity—assuming that people *are*

1. Dominiak, *The Falling of Dusk*, 27.

in fact seeking unity—is worked out among individuals within the broader gathering of the church, in the renewed temple context of the body of Christ.

Christ, as King, possesses the "land" in which this new-kingdom-context of dwelling together occurs. We may view the idea of the land in a figurative sense in this case, especially given that the very basis of the new kingdom is *figured* in Christ, and Christians would of course also say *pre*figured in the Old Testament. A key aspect of the nature of that land is in itself the *effect* of our participation within it. For this reason it is fitting that Ephesians 2:20 does not say that Christ alone fulfils the role of providing *any form* of foundation whatsoever. It says, instead, that Christ is the cornerstone, the principal foundation, but that this also allows some foundational significance to the lives of apostles and prophets. During my time at theological college I remember hearing it quoted from someone—I forget exactly whom now—that a house built on living stones is bound to be experienced at times as somewhat *shaky*. Shakiness, and shaken-ness, as we have already seen, are in themselves notable Advent themes. How relations might be properly established or reestablished in the face of individual differences in such a context is certainly something that any ministerial training should touch upon at some point, and perhaps in practice an entire module may even be attached to it, in line with ongoing reflective practice. Differences of *perspective* are likewise a big topic in Dominiak's highly recommendable book, being in many respects the "raw material," not least in psychological terms, for an informed striving towards establishing, reestablishing, and holding together proper relations within the created order.

Exploring the metaphor of monarchy a bit further, we might reflect on the fact that allegiance to a monarch or head of state often involves something being said, or even sworn in some cases, concerning what it is to be a good citizen. When the kingdom in question is that of Christ the citizenship is that of heaven (Phil 3:20) and "with the saints" (Eph 2:19). This is memorably reinforced in Hebrews 12:22–24, assuring the recipients that they "have come to Mount Zion and to the city of the living God, the heavenly Jerusalem . . . to the assembly of the firstborn . . . to the spirits of the righteous made perfect, and to Jesus, the mediator of a new covenant, and to the sprinkled blood that speaks a better word than the blood of Abel." This proclamation does two very obvious things: firstly, it puts the theological birth status of all concerned on the same level, regardless of individual difference, held in perfect relation to each other; secondly, it reminds us of that blood which speaks of great cost, of the signing of a covenant, and of a divine communication—speaking "a better word." In Genesis 4:10 the Lord tells Cain that his brother Abel's "blood is crying out to me from the ground!" The Hebrew word for ground is again *a'damah*, so the blood in question cries out from where God fashioned humanity, but a ground which has now become compromised (cf. Gen 3:17–19). Cain is therefore told that he is "cursed from the ground" and that "it will no longer yield" such that Cain "will be a fugitive and a wanderer" (Gen 4:11–12), which reinforces the *nomadic* status of humanity's existence already hinted in Genesis 3:23–24.

In the Hebrews text the ground is transformed into a new foundation by the "better word" that is spoken. Humanity needs to learn what it is to be, or to become, newly and properly human in Christ, participating *in* the grounding that has afforded this very possibility. The activity of orienting to this new life will feel challenging and "shaky" at times, since, as an Advent people especially, we are acclimatizing together regarding what is involved in being a new citizen. The right and proper relations, like the church's unity, are to be *discovered* and *discerned*, and also *appreciated as a gift*—being in themselves neither a static "summary of principles" bracketed off from the practicality of formation, nor that which we ourselves construct purely by our own initiative and self-assertion. This is something I have often needed to remind myself, as well as trying to emphasize the fact especially in the Week of Prayer for Christian Unity each January.

In terms of the *coming towards* theme of Advent, the principal sense is that in which the "towards" indicates God-towards-us, which is in itself what enables the complementary sense of us-towards-God. There is a related sense, however, in which it also requires us to come towards *one another* in the, at times, complex negotiation of our collective formation and transformed citizenship. There may be many unexpected opportunities to do this that come to us at sudden moments and in complex situations, some of which may go unrecognized or unused. We do, however, perhaps stand a far better chance of a more fruitful recognition and response if we commit to bearing in mind that the correctness or properness of the relations involved is not something which is specifically *im*posed by us. Rather, it is according to the properness and righteousness of Christ the King that we may come to the increasing realization and appreciation that the gathering or assembly of which we are part is intricately *com*posed, in and as the new kingdom which Christ brings.

Reflection 23

O Emmanuel

O Emmanuel, our King and Lawgiver,
the Desire of all Nations, and their Saviour:
Come and save us, O Lord our God.'

(cf. Isa 7:14; 33:22; 1 Tim 4:10)

To begin with, let us turn again to Isaiah, in this case Isaiah 7:10–15, in which the prefiguring of the Emmanuel figure is given by the prophet.

> Again the Lord spoke to Ahaz, saying, Ask a sign of the Lord your God; let it be deep as Sheol or high as heaven. But Ahaz said, I will not ask, and I will not put the Lord to the test. Then Isaiah [in the Hebrew just "he"] said: 'Hear then, O house of David! Is it too little for you to weary mortals, that you weary my God also? Therefore the Lord himself will give you a sign. Look, the young woman is with child and shall bear a son, and shall name him Immanuel. He shall eat curds and honey by the time he knows how to refuse the evil and choose the good.'

This passage has been subject to much commentary, but overall it is perhaps the mention of *knowing* in the final verse that constitutes the most important aspect for today's reflection. The curds might seem to be placed in poetic parallel with "the evil" and the honey with "the good." Those familiar with the Exodus story might well think here of the "land flowing with milk and honey" that was promised to the Israelites (Exod 3:8, 17; 33:3; Num 14:8; Deut 26:9; Ezek 20:6). In the context of the quoted Isaiah passage the milk has seemingly curdled and, in this respect, the tasting experience is somewhat mixed.[1] Given the subsequent mention of good and evil we might compare this experience to the entanglement of the wheat and the weeds in the famous parable Jesus tells in Matthew 13:24–30. This also helps, of course, to place the idea of the Promised Land in a figurative context, seeing its true fulfilment as much in terms of mental and spiritual place as physical context. The mind in question plays an active and discerning role in distinguishing and in moving towards a context where, ultimately, only good is actively expressed.

Knowledgeable discernment is called for, and the child to be born is here promised to bring in such true discernment, right from early youth. In Luke's Gospel we hear of those witnessing the boy Jesus, just when he is coming of age in the society of the time, being noted as "amazed at his understanding and his answers" as he is found "sitting among the teachers" in the temple (Luke 2:46–47). A few verses earlier we are told that Jesus "grew and became strong, filled with wisdom; and the favour of God was upon him" (Luke 2:40), and, shortly after his remarkable show of understanding in the temple, we hear added to this statement that "Jesus increased in wisdom and in years, and in divine *and* [my italics] human favour" (Luke 2:52).

Early childhood is the most spectacular of the various developmental phases in life, in which so much happens within a relatively short time-span. As Jesus was fully human as well as fully divine, he is no exception in this sense. The child mentioned in the Isaiah text is immersed in the physical practice of discernment in a material context, and with startling efficiency by the tone of the

1. In fact, the translation "sour milk" does occur in the New English Translation, or indeed "curdled milk" in the Complete Jewish Bible (translations can readily be compared at biblegateway.com).

text, searching out and "tasting" reality as encountered by human nature *and* in particular in its image-bearing relation to divinity. In Psalm 34:8 we hear the exhortation, "O taste and see that the LORD is good; happy are those who take refuge in him." Both the *form* and the *result* of the searching out, the tasting, the recognizing, and the appreciating of such refuge are uniquely expressed in Christ. He is a new focus of unity, a basis of restoration for human nature, ultimately even of transfiguration, and hence why the Emmanuel figure is to be the hope of all the nations as considered from a New Testament perspective.

1 Timothy 4:10 talks of the "end" towards which "we toil," including through struggling or suffering reproach. In the famous hymn *O Come, O Come, Emmanuel* we hear, in the opening verse, of a "captive Israel that mourns in lonely exile" and the fact that this continues to be sung by Christians, after Christ's resurrection, shows that part of our Advent appreciation *now* is that there remains a sense that not everything is yet brought to its final resting place. We remain somewhat foreign to a *full* vision, awareness, and appreciation of our place as occupiers of the fulfilment of the Promised Land in Christ, presently seeing only "dimly" (or "in a riddle" in the Greek) as 1 Corinthians 13:12 reminds us. Occupation of the "land" in question is a guided process of reorientation, remembering what was said previously about the orientational significance of the temple. Emmanuel means "God with us," and is the Advent phrase and figure that most emphasizes the sharing of our human nature in the new temple context, deliberately placed just before the eve of the Christmas season.

In Hebrews 4:15 we are reminded that we have "a high priest" who can "sympathize with our weaknesses . . . who in every respect has been tested as we are, yet without sin." So powerful is the victory of the divine-human union in Christ that a new created order is brought in through a new temple in which the aforementioned filling of the temple by the Lord's robe in the vision of Isaiah 6:1 is re-presented in the context of the flesh of Christ and our sharing in his body as the church. The Isaiah vision implicitly suggests that the feet of the Lord touch the temple floor, and Psalm 110:1

mentions the famous phrase, "Sit at my right hand until I make your enemies your footstool," which is further cited in Hebrews 10:12–13 as a description of the nature of Christ's glory, not least as high priest. The Nicene Creed also of course speaks of Jesus "seated at the right hand of the Father," and it is clear why this accompanies an acclamation of Christ's ascension.

Elsewhere we hear the LORD asking the question as to what form of house humanity could possibly build for divinity, given that, "Heaven is my throne and the earth is my footstool" (Isa 66:1), an aspect also reflected in the image of the hem of the Lord's robe filling the temple while he sits in high majesty upon his throne. In the risen and ascended Christ we have one for and at whose feet a *new earth* is brought to bear as a transformed footstool, and those who were previously alien, "far off," being in some sense or another not properly oriented to the Way of God and falling "short of the glory of God" (Eph 2:12–13; Rom 3:23), are "brought near by the blood of Christ" (Eph 2:13). In him the feet and the head are connected in the body that is the church, raising up that which is redeemed such that it is no longer *of* the world despite still being *in* the world.

The Emmanuel figure draws us to *re-con-figure*, especially in the sense of *newly figuring together* in this case, our view of ourselves as being made anew. We are drawn to appreciate more clearly the true Image of God in Christ, according to which the "motioning" of our human nature finds a clear and distinct resonance with that of divinity, through that great divine-human union that is the Incarnation. As the last of the antiphons, this one brings our Advent journey to the theme of *becoming*, something inseparable from the accompanying sense of God *with* us, carrying with it an inviting open-endedness. The directed motioning of Advent paves the way for, hopefully, a genuinely fresh acknowledgement of the great, history-turning transition that *is* the Incarnation, accommodating the context and challenges of our existence in all their many dimensions. Not least, it brings in a new and transfigured pattern of *relation* between those aspects of our existence that we, certainly as individuals, may tend to think of as our inner and outer senses of reality. A deeper sense of unity is to be found within the motioning lying at the core of Advent's richness.

Advent points not to some far-off prospect but to a reinvigorated sense of God-with-us, mysterious and pervasive while at the same time involving a shaking and a transfiguring—a directed turning and a glorious returning in the risen and ascended Christ. It is now time to hold this Advent perspective high and to ask what our journey into another Christmas Eve really means if we truly view it through a multidimensional Advent lens.

Reflection 24

The Manifold Witness

In the hymn *Great is Thy Faithfulness* we hear of the idea of being part of a "manifold witness" in which nature, in the broadest sense, participates. The verse from which these words are taken refers to the motioning of celestial bodies and the cycle of the seasons—images contouring a broad-brushstroke picture of "nature" in this case. Nature contributes the many dimensions and dynamics involved in the manifold witness in question. If one thing in particular has stuck out from these reflections then I hope very much that it is the sheer variety, the *entire manifold* of dynamic themes which are connected with, and held together within, Advent. As an Advent people we are a witnessing people, and the manifold nature of that witness itself bears witness to the many ways in which the manifold in question can become *manifest* among us as things *un*fold.

This is already one link with Christmas. If by any chance you are actually reading this on Christmas Eve then I am in many ways flattered as I know what a hectic time this day can be. Wrapping presents is likely to be an activity that many will be engaged in at this time, but we should remember that, when we come to *un*wrap the gift of Christ, this does *not* involve tearing away a superficial covering in order to see what is "really" within. *Unfolding* is therefore a better description of what we do, or should aim to do, with the *entire* gift that Christmas and everything that *follows* represents theologically. Nothing is torn off and wasted in this case. The manifold quality of the gift is unfolded, with prayer, thanksgiving, and all due Advent attentiveness and hope.

In mathematical circles the word manifold is often used, especially in the field known as topology. Topology is basically the study of the holistic property of a space—how it is *globally connected*. As an example, a particular form can be bent, like shaping a piece of plasticine, without altering the topology, just as long as it is not torn or punctured at any point or along any line, since that would change the nature of the overall connectedness. There is a certain elastic flexibility involved in the very concept of topology in this case, rather like the London Underground Map in which the strict geographical locations of the stations are not given, since that would make the 2D means of representation too tricky. Instead, there is a re-forming of the layout that maintains the overall connectedness while using the flexibility, the plasticity if you like, to move the relative positions of each station into a configuration that allows all to be seen together without obstruction, and the connecting routes clearly to be traced.

In a sense, I would suggest that to map our journey, or possible journeys, through Advent follows a similar principle. There is a *dynamic flexibility* to how we might express and view the manifold richness of God's motioning towards us and among us, while still respecting how it is connected overall—unfolding rather than tearing. There is clearly a connectedness between the various major themes involved in these reflections. Such themes have included time, both in terms of the *direction* of viewpoint and in terms of the *rate* of change involved; memory; hope and active expectancy; transition; opening; alertness; and, not least, our developing inward vision and sense of the eschatological, of the anticipated fullness of the unfolding. Furthermore, there is a *narrative* connectedness between many of the key figures that Advent emphasizes, as well as a connectedness among the antiphons, not least since they all ultimately refer to the same Person—the Second Person of the Trinity in becoming flesh and dwelling among us.

Some of these connections are so obvious that we are unlikely either to consider or to risk breaking them up, but other more subtle connections may require care and attentiveness *not* to tear apart and accidentally to disrupt the overall "topology" of Advent in so doing. There is, in addition to all this, one other *living* connection that is, realistically, both more under our control than anything else and yet simultaneously hardest, at times, to keep responsible track on. I refer, of course, to the connection *to us* as individuals. Advent has been emphasized as a shared enterprise here because, among other things, we need the help of others to be an Advent people in the proper way. We require interaction with others—others who are also consciously striving to pay attention to the call to a collective journey—in order to keep the manner of our own involvement and connectedness appropriate and responsible. We clearly do not know in advance who might say what, do what, think what, realize what, or indeed *when* they might do so, but we *can* be sure that the roles played by others will in some way influence the manner in which we learn to seek our place in the journey of faith and our connectedness to the Advent themes noted in these reflections. Once again, others will inevitably have some "adverbial" influence in this respect, recalling what was said in the theological introduction to this book.

The opening of the final door of the Advent calendar is almost bound to involve a manger scene, but to open it is not to leave the relevance of Advent behind. The manger scene is not a stopping point indicating the end of one seasonal journey and marking the beginning of a totally different one. It is a place emphasizing awe, contemplative adoration, and, above all, the power and meaning of *presence*. The small gathering around the crib in the biblical story sees the drawing together of many different but representative presences. We find Mary, Joseph, shepherds, wise men, and very probably farm animals. There were almost certainly others of whom we don't hear explicitly, but wondered what was going on. In fact, there is something of a hint of this in the wording of Luke 2:18. All these represent different aspects of society or different individual roles and perspectives, and even a wider representation on the part of non-human life. Because the context of this presence seems so simple, its diversity and meaningfulness could easily be overlooked. The common factor resides in the center of gravity that draws the attention of those present, attention on the one lying in the manger, but not to the exclusion of other interaction among those present, such as the shepherds telling the story of their encounter with the angel of the Lord in the fields—words which, as we have acknowledged, are met by the treasuring and pondering of Mary.

Whatever your concerns *today*, whether you read this in Advent or at any other time of the year, and whatever your hopes and expectations of the future, given the opportunities that it holds or the challenges and obligations that it imposes, it remains the case that the bigger picture highlighted by Advent, a season of enduring significance, is there to help us, and to help us *together*. I wrote the first draft of this text during Advent 2024 and at that time it had not yet gone anywhere near a publisher. It was clearly not possible to say at that point when it might be read or by whom, and I was, and still am, all too aware that a lot could change in the world between the time of writing and the time of reading—changes that may well be of great concern to a large number of people. In many respects, however, this makes it all the more important to emphasize the Advent themes considered here as themes whose relevance will *not* change but which are there to support, draw hope, and where necessary challenge, in a spirit focused on the surety that there is always more than seems presently the case.

This is not only an invitation carefully and prayerfully to unfold the manifold nature of that to which we are called collectively to witness, but also a reminder of the *partial* nature of our present perspective. Our perspective will inevitably be stretched along various directions and dimensions as our life progresses and as it, along with the connected perspectives of others, becomes more appreciably *embedded within the same manifold* to which it witnesses. That is the basis for a motioning towards a *final sharing* of a perspective far more glorious than any of us could possibly have accommodated alone.

I hope that these reflections, and their combination as a complete book, have allowed the reader to reflect on the many influential dimensions of the dynamic underpinning of Advent on our contemporary lives, as we all continue to experience our individual impressions both *of* and *along* a journey that many have trodden before us and others will experience after us.

Bibliography

Aland, Black et al. *Novum Testamentum Graece*. 27th ed. Stuttgart: Deutsche Bibelgesellschaft, 2001.

Allison, Dale C., Jr. "Matthew." In *The Oxford Bible Commentary*, edited by J. Barton and J. Muddiman, 844–886. Oxford: Oxford University Press, 2001.

Cross, F. L., and E. A. Livingstone, eds. *The Oxford Dictionary of the Christian Church*. 3rd ed. Oxford: Oxford University Press, 2005.

Davidson, Benjamin. *The Analytical Hebrew and Chaldee Lexicon*. Peabody, MA: Hendrickson, 2007.

Dominiak, Paul. *The Falling of Dusk*. London: Bloomsbury, 2022.

Hastings, Adrian. "Prophecy." In *The Oxford Companion to Christian Thought*, edited by Adrian Hastings et al., 568–570. Oxford: Oxford University Press, 2000.

Liddell, Henry George, and Robert Scott. *Greek-English Lexicon: With a Revised Supplement*. Oxford: Clarendon, 1996.

Loughlin, Gerard. "Time." In *The Oxford Companion to Christian Thought*, edited by Adrian Hastings et al., 707–709. Oxford: Oxford University Press, 2000.

Mayne, Michael. *Pray, Love, Remember*. London: Darton, Longman and Todd, 2005.

Neale, John M., trans., and Thomas Helmore, music ed. *Hymnal Noted: Parts I and II*. London: Novello, Ewer and Co., 1851.

Nicholl, Donald. *Holiness*. London: Darton, Longman and Todd, 2004.

Sayers, Dorothy L. *The Mind of the Maker*. New York: HarperSanFrancisco, 1987.

The British and Foreign Bible Society, *The Holy Scriptures of the Old Testament: Hebrew and English*. 1996.

Williams, Rowan. *The Edge of Words: God and the Habits of Human Language*. London: Bloomsbury, 2014.

———. *Open to Judgement: Sermons and Addresses*. London: Darton, Longman and Todd, 2003.

www.ingramcontent.com/pod-product-compliance
Lightning Source LLC
LaVergne TN
LVHW012333100826
845148LV00017B/2159

* 9 7 9 8 3 8 5 2 7 7 4 2 1 *